NOTHING TRUER
THAN TRUTH

VERO NIHIL VERIVS

Nothing Truer
Than Truth

Being the life and times
of Edward de Vere,
17th Earl of Oxford, Viscount Bulbec,
Lord Sandford and Badlesmere,
sometime known as
WILLIAM SHAKE-SPEARE

VERO NIHIL VERIVS

Darrol Blake

Riverhouse Press

ISBN: 978-1-9161947-0-0-

First published in the UK by
Riverhouse Press
riverhousepress1@gmail.com

Cover design, layout and typesetting by Helm Information
amandahelm@uwclub.net

Print management by Guy Eve
guyeve61@gmail.com

Printed and bound in Great Britain

Contents

Illustrations

Introduction

*N*othing *Truer Than Truth* is my play performed at the Overground Theatre in Kingston-upon-Thames from 24th May to 11th June 1977 which traces the life of Edward de Vere, the 17th Earl of Oxford, from his birth in 1550 until the 1590s. It makes the case that he was the Bard by using passages of the poetry published in his own name and extracts from his plays and sonnets published later under his pen-name "William Shakespeare", adopted for the first time in 1593 when the first of his two narrative poems, *Venus and Adonis*, appeared.

In the 1970s I was a freelance drama director on numerous drama series for the BBC when I was asked by an actor, Nigel Bradshaw, to write a one-man show about Rupert Brooke, to be performed by him at the Overground Theatre. This I did, and *Sweet Wine of Youth,* a life of Rupert Brooke taken from his letters and poems, was performed there in 1976; Nigel unfortunately had other acting commitments and Brian Stirner took the part. I subsequently revised the play for television and directed it for the BBC in 1979 with Simon Shepherd in the title role and a large cast including Rachel Kempson and Richard Pascoe.

I was interested in the Shakespeare authorship debate and in particular the candidacy of Edward de Vere, and the highly rewarding task of trawling through Brooke's poems and letters gave me the idea of doing the same exercise with De Vere/Shakespeare. It was an impulse, whim or conceit, but it would nonetheless confirm the truth of the matter. Designing the play as I was writing was easy as I had been a BBC set designer and was used to "no money" productions. We gathered a cast of professional actors as shown in the Overground Theatre Programme (see the inset photographic section) all playing for bus fares, literally!

Damien Thomas (Edward) I had met on the only feature film I had worked on, *The Message*; Alan Bryce, who ran the theatre, stepped up to play several roles; Colin McCormack (Knyvet/Golding/Yorke) had worked with the Bristol Old Vic, the Royal Shakespeare Company and many other theatres; Will Boyde (the Earl of Southampton), I had seen in a production of *Journey's End*; Anne Jameson (Queen Elizabeth) was married to the well-known character actor, Brian Pringle, who was a friend; and my wife, Anne Cunningham, played Edward's mother in Act One and Ann Vavasor in Act Two - not only that but she came with me, searching out costume items from local amateur groups; and she made ruffs and lots of candles - the ruffs being in short supply because Londoners were dressing up in Elizabethan costumes for the Queen's Silver Jubilee.

The principals were dressed by Berman's, while the rest of the cast came from auditions in Kingston. An American, Rick Fisher, later a West-end lighting designer, was the Stage Manager, Michael Poynor designed the lighting and directed the fights, and Colin and Damien, who had been at RADA, were right in their element. The play was well-attended and received good reviews (see Appendix A) and it would have run for longer, but for the fact that the theatre had another production booked to commence the following week.

Appendix B identifies the main passages in the text which I took from the De Vere/Shakespeare poems and plays, and my fellow De Vere Society member, Oliver Kinsey, has kindly added a postscript (Appendix C).

While this play is entirely mine, I must thank Amanda Helm for the type-setting and Oliver for the initial idea and seeing the project through.

Darrol Blake
July 2019

1. Cast Photograph From left: Gary Hope (Arundel/John Lyly), Graham Padden (Philip Sidney), the Founder and Director of the Overground Theatre Alan Bryce (Nicholas Dawtrey/Gabriel Harvey), Annabel Giles (Anne Cecil/Elizabeth Vere), in the centre Elizabeth Jameson (the Queen), William Boyde (the Earl of Southampton), Anne Cunningham (Margaret, Countess of Oxford/ Ann Vavasor), Anthony Chambers (Will Shaxper/ Ambassador to France), Colin McCormack (Arthur Golding/Rowland Yorke/ Thomas Knyvet). Missing: Damien Thomas (Edward de Vere) and Dennis Edwards (William Cecil).

ix

The Overground's next production is PEIFFER'S PEOPLE by Jules Peiffer. Repeating the formula which proved so successful with YOURE A GOOD MAN CHARLIE BROWN, we present another revue based on the drawings of an American cartoonist. However, there the difference starts. PEIFFER'S PEOPLE is New York revue at its best—chronicling the hilarious fantasising of Bernard Mergendiler, supercool Huey and a whole throng of New York's weirdest and funniest.

In the all-American cast are ANNIE-LEE TAYLOR, ZHIVILA ROCHE, DIANA VAN FOSSEN, HARRY DITSON EDWARD FRENCH and DAVID MONICO.

PEIFFER'S PEOPLE will be directed by MICHAEL POYNOR.

****

When PEIFFER'S PEOPLE closes on July 2nd, the Overground will close for two months for our summer break. We shall re-open early in September with a play yet to be announced.

****

DARROL BLAKE, director and devisor of NOTHING TRUER THAN TRUTH has also directed THE GOLDEN PATHWAY ANNUAL at the Overground as well as his own SWEET WINE OF YOUTH, about the poet Rupert Brooke. Darrol's main work however is as a freelance TV director, where his credits include THE ONEDIN LINE, THE VENTURE THE REGIMENT, DOOMWATCH, CROSS-ROADS and many others.

ALAN BRYCE is co-artistic director of the Overground. He trained in New York and worked with the Second City Improvisation Theatre in Chicago and at the Weston Playhouse in Vermont, before returning to the UK where he worked in Rep at Belfast and Sheffield. His play THE TROUBLE WITH ANTS was performed at the Traverse Theatre, Edinburgh.

ANTHONY CHAMBERS has just finished the opening season at the new Rep in Southampton. Has also worked at Pitlochry, Brighton, Cheltenham & Watford. Played 'the son' in SIX CHARACTERS IN SEARCH OF AN AUTHOR for TV. Other TV includes ANGELS, HADLEIGH and the DICK EMERY SHOW.

****

We would like to thank for their assistance with this production:

BENTALLS

CHIESMANS

CHESSINGTON ZOO

TEDDINGTON THEATRE CLUB

Plo Kingdom
County Players
Andy Wilkinson
Mike Wyres
Masque Dance Theatre Co.
Leslie Limberg
Richard Denton
Anne Blake
Lynettre Coomber
and
DAVID BEARD

NOTHING TRUER THAN TRUTH

OVERGROUND THEATRE

NOTHING TRUER THAN TRUTH

devised directed and designed by
DARROL BLAKE

lighting designed by
MICHAEL POYNOR

Arthur Golding...COLIN McCORMACK
Edward aged 12...RAINER HERSH or
                 DAVID EVANS

William Cecil
(Lord Burghley)..DENNIS EDWARDS
Countess of
       Oxford....ANN CUNNINGHAM
Edward de Vere...DAMIEN THOMAS
Philip Sydney....GRAHAM PADDEN
Ann Cecil, later
Countess of
       Oxford...ANNABEL GILES
Earl of Arundel..GARY HOPE
Queen Elisabeth..ANNE JAMESON
Nicholas Dawtrey.ALAN BRYCE
Ambassador to
       France....ANTHONY CHAMBERS
Rowland Yorke....COLIN McCORMACK
Miranda/Audrey...ANDREW BOAGEY or
                 PAUL PENN-SIMKIN
John Lyly........GARY HOPE
Ariel............RAINER HERSH or
                 DAVID EVANS
Gabriel Harvey...ALAN BRYCE
Thomas Kryvet....COLIN McCORMACK
Ann Vavasor......ANNE CUNNINGHAM
Will Shaxper.....ANTHONY CHAMBERS
Earl of
   Southampton...WILLIAM BOYDE
****
Choreography.....JANE WINEARLS
Stage Management.RICK FISHER
                 NIKKI WORSFOLD
                 DERINA DINKIN
****

For the OVERGROUND THEATRE

Artistic Directors
          ....ALAN BRYCE
              MARIA RICCIO

Associate Director
          ...TONY HEYWOOD
Front of House...SANDY LINCOLN
Graphics........NICK JENKINS
****

The Overground Theatre receives
financial assistance from the
Arts Council of Great Britain
****

COLIN McCORMACK has worked
with the Bristol Old Vic, the
Royal Shakespeare Company, the
Royal Lyceum Theatre in Edinburgh, the Nottingham Playhouse
and the Welsh National Theatre
among many others. Colin lives
nearby in Kingston.

DENNIS EDWARDS has worked in
most repertory theatres throughout the country. His favourite
parts include Mathews in PENNY
FOR A SONG, Mr Frank in THE
DIARY OF ANNE FRANK and Soames
in GETTING MARRIED. He recently
appeared as Mr Bray in NICHOLAS
NICKLEBY.

ANNE CUNNINGHAM is best known
for her work on television as
with 3 young children she has
been restricted in her work in
the theatre. However, last year
she played the lead in WAIT
UNTIL DARK at Guildford. Recent
TV includes GENERAL HOSPITAL
and THE RISE AND FALL OF
REGINALD PERRIN.

DAMIEN THOMAS was trained at RADA
and has worked extensively in
repertory and television - most
recently in THE EXPERT, WARSHIP
and 1990. He is currently featured
in THE MESSAGE an epic based on
the life of the prophet Mohammed
& was recently seen in the Monday
late night horror movie TWINS OF
EVIL. Damien can be seen in the
next Sinbad adventure, soon to be
on general release.

GRAHAM PADDEN was born in Worcest-
er Park. He trained at the Bristol
Old Vic Theatre School and has
worked at the Liverpool Playhouse
Chester and the Victoria theatre,
Stoke on Trent. Graham played the
title role in Dr FAUSTUS at Perth
last year as well as appearing in
THE NORMAN CONQUESTS and MAN AND
SUPERMAN.

GARY HOPE will be familiar to
Overground audiences - he has appeared here before in SWEET WINE OF
YOUTH and EDEN. He has also worked
in all the major repertory theatres
throughout the country. He recently
toured the UK as Noel Coward in
COWARDY CUSTARD. TV includes James
Stephen in THE FIGHT AGAINST SLAVERY
and Peregrine Sutton in GENERAL
HOSPITAL.

ANNE JAMESON began acting as an 11-
year old in the film NO ROOM AT THE
INN and was seen recently in Ken
Russell's THE BOYFRIEND..She was
last seen at the Savoy in LLOYD
GEORGE KNEW MY FATHER and has made
many television appearances. Her
new series, THE PAPER LADS will be
shown in September on ITV.

xi

2. The Queen (Anne Jameson), the Earl of Arundel (Gary Hope), William Cecil, Lord Burghley (Dennis Edwards) and Guards (William Boyde and Rick Fisher).

Arundel, on his knees, is about to be dragged by the guards to the Tower: pp. 27/28.

3. **Edward de Vere (Damien Thomas) and Ann Vavasor (Anne Cunningham).**

Edward and Ann
together speak
De Vere's 'Echoes'
poem: pp. 35/36.

4. **Edward de Vere (Damien Thomas), Will Shaxper (Anthony Chambers) and Audrey (Andrew Boagey or Paul Penn-Simkin).**

Having embraced Will as "a very excellent factotum and supernumerary actor" in his company, Edward is inspired to improvise the forest scene in *As You Like It* – "It is meat and drink to me to see a clown..." Act V sc.1, with Will, the country wench Audrey, and himself as Touchstone, the court jester: pp. 43/46.

5. Edward de Vere (Damien Thomas), Henry Wriothesley, the Earl of Southampton (William Boyde) and Elizabeth Vere (Annabel Giles).

As the betrothed couple, Henry (17) and Elizabeth (15) chat, her father Edward (40) reads Shakespeare's Sonnet No 2, "When forty winters shall beseige thy brow ..." Page 55.

6. Edward de Vere
(Damien Thomas),
Henry Wriothesley,
the Earl of Southampton
(William Boyde).

Henry reads out aloud
the author's dedication to
himself of the Shakespeare
poem, *The Rape of Lucrece*:
pp. 55/56.

Nothing Truer Than Truth

VERO NIHIL VERIVS

Nothing Truer Than Truth

Characters

EDWARD de VERE (aged 12)
ARTHUR GOLDING (about 40)
MARGARET, **Countess of Oxford** (mid thirties)
SIR WILLIAM CECIL (afterwards **Lord Burghley**) (50–70)
JOHN CLAPHAM (Sir William's secretary) (late 20s)
ANNE CECIL (afterwards **Countess of Oxford**) (aged 15)
CHARLES ARUNDEL (late 20s)
QUEEN ELIZABETH I (40–55)
EDWARD de VERE, 17th Earl of Oxford (22–42)
YOUNG LORD
CAPT. NICHOLAS DAWTREY (early thirties but fat)
PHILIP SIDNEY (22–30)
TWO TRAVELLERS
TWO THIEVES
DR. DALE (**English Ambassador to Paris**) (about 40)
ROWLAND YORKE (about 40)
MAIDS OF HONOUR
TWO BOY ACTORS 'Miranda' /'Ariel'/'Audrey' (12–14)
GABRIEL HARVEY (about 30)
ANN VAVASOR (early 30s)
THOMAS KNYVET (about 45–50)
TWO HENCHMEN
JOHN LYLY (early 30s)
THREE ACTORS IN OXFORD'S COMPANY
WILL SHAXPER (22)
EARL of SOUTHAMPTON (18–20)
ELIZABETH VERE (15)
HORACE VERE (45)

Act One

BLACKOUT. *Fanfare then spotlight on de Vere arms with motto plainly seen.* VERO NIHIL VERIUS. *Lights fade in on* **EDWARD**, *aged 12, seated at writing table L. surrounded by books and papers. His pen scratches away.* **NARRATOR** (**ARTHUR GOLDING**) *appears near him.*

NARRATOR: (*to audience*) Edward de Vere, Viscount Bulbec. (*walks round boy who ignores him.*) His father, the Sixteenth Earl of Oxford, hereditary Lord Great Chamberlain of England, is a man greatly honoured in this country. The continuance of his family in the male line and its possession of an Earldom for more than five and a half centuries have made its name a household word.

(**EDWARD** *puts down his pen and reads what he has been writing – it is several pages long.*)

EDWARD: (*Reading*) The Stage of the World! (*he looks at Golding to see if he approves*) wherein is made a large discourse of man's miseries, and also of many vices that at this present day reign in all estates of the Earth. First book. Many ancient, both Greek, Latin and barbarous philosophers having diligently considered all sorts of living creatures, have exclaimed that among all those that breathe, or have any being upon the Earth, there is not one so miserable as man. (*He stops to correct something.*)

NARRATOR: (*to audience*) His mother is Margaret Golding, my half sister. Oh! (*introducing himself*) Arthur Golding, Latin tutor to the young Viscount.

EDWARD: (*Reading*) Lo how poor Plutarch, after he had wearied himself in the contemplation of man's misery, would willingly have desired never to have been or at least

3

to have been transformed into some brute beast, by reason of the excessive faults which he found with the vices of men. (*Barking dogs, footsteps and male and female voices heard offstage.*) My father!

GOLDING: (*motioning for him to sit down again*) The Ovid translation – The Epilogue.

EDWARD: (*opening a book at the end, translating with little difficulty*) And now I have completed a work which neither the anger of Jove, nor fire, nor sword, nor devouring Time, will be able to destroy. Let that day, which has no power but over my body put an end to my uncertain life when it will. Yet in the better part of me (*to Golding*) *Parte tamen meliore mei* (*laughter and noise off*) I shall be raised immortal above the lofty stars and indelible shall be my name.

GOLDING: Good . . . the better part of me. Um (*he dismisses him*). The boy is precociously learned . . . (*Edward runs off C.*) I have laboured long and hard to translate the works of Ovid and my humble version of the *Metamorphoses* will soon be published . . . (*music begins off*) Castle Hedingham is full and festive now. The Uncles have gathered: the Earl of Surrey, famous for his verse, my Lord Sheffield, the writer of a book of sonnets in the Italian style. And this evening there will be an entertainment; music, plays and juggling by my Lord Oxford's own company of actors. Why? Because the Queen is here. Lord Oxford has been negotiating a marriage with the son of the King of Sweden but she will none of him, tho' all men would have her wedded and . . . But she has a shrewd wit and is not yet thirty. (*Music up to climax and lights fade as he exits.*)

[**Blackout**] (*Music ends on ominous note as lights fade in.* **SIR WILLIAM CECIL** *enters and sits at writing table R.*)

(**GOLDING** *re-enters dressed for travelling with a weeping Countess of Oxford. A servant holds a travelling box and a lantern.*)

GOLDING: A year later and all is changed. The Earl is dead and as the Seventeenth Earl of Oxford is in his minority he becomes a royal ward, with all his lands and incomes in the hands of Sir William Cecil, Secretary of State and Master of the Wards and Liveries, by means whereof he became rich.

(**EDWARD** *now Earl of Oxford has appeared during this, he is cloaked and walks slowly to his mother.*)

COUNTESS: In delivering my son from me I bury a second husband.

EDWARD: And I in going, madam, weep o'er my father's death anew; but I must attend Her Majesty's command, to whom I am now in ward, evermore in subjection.

COUNTESS: Be thou blest Edward and succeed thy father in manners as in shape! Thy blood and virtue contend for empire in thee, and thy goodness share with thy birthright! Love all, trust a few, do wrong to none, be able for thine enemy rather in power than use, and keep thy friend under thine own life's key; be checked for silence, but never tax'd for speech. What heaven more will, that thee may furnish, and my prayer pluck down, fall on thy head! Farewell.

(**EDWARD** *slowly exits.*)

'Tis an unseasoned courtier, Good Arthur advise him.

GOLDING: He cannot want the best that shall attend his love.

COUNTESS: Heaven bless him! (*Golding leaves her.*) Farewell Edward.

(*As the light slowly fades from* **COUNTESS**, **CECIL** *is still spotlit and* **GOLDING** *crosses to a spot near him.*)

5

GOLDING: My sister remarried soon afterwards, one Charles Tyrrell. The funeral bakemeats did coldly furnish the marriage table. Lord Oxford received his degree from Cambridge at 14 and 2 years later was made Master of Arts at Oxford. At 17 he was, with Philip Sidney and a cousin John Manners, admitted to Gray's Inn to study law for 3 years.

(**ANNE CECIL** *aged 14 enters and goes to her father.*)

Within the walls of Gray's Inn Cecil had grouped the most brilliant young men of the day .... Afterwards they remained friends when –

(*Lights up on* **PHILIP SIDNEY, EDWARD DE VERE** *and* **CHARLES ARUNDEL** *in Edward's rooms in the Savoy.*)

Edward, already a patron of poets and writers, took rooms for them in a tenement off the Strand called the Savoy.

(**GOLDING**'s *light fades as* **EDWARD** *begins.*)

EDWARD: Were I a King, I might command content,
Were I obscure, unknown would be my cares,
And were I dead, no thoughts should me torment,
Nor words nor wrongs, nor love, nor hate, nor fears.
A doubtful choice of three things one to crave
A kingdom or a cottage or a grave.

(**SIDNEY,** *not to be outdone, extemporises.*)

SIDNEY: Wert thou a king, yet not command content
Since empire none thy mind could yet suffice,
Wert thou obscure, still cares would thee torment,
But wert thou dead, all care and sorrow dies.
An easy choice of three things one to crave
No kingdom, nor a cottage, but a grave.

(*They laugh but there is an edge of rivalry between them.*)

6

EDWARD: Philip, I mean to publish these works, give me of thy best.

SIDNEY: There are so many courtly makers, will you collect all their scribblings?

EDWARD: In these days poets as well as poesie are become subjects of scorn and derision. Who so is studious in the art and shows himself excellent in it, they call him fantastical and lightheaded.

ARUNDEL: Of such among the nobility or gentry as to be very well seen in the making of poesie, it is come to such a pass that they are loath to be known of their skill.

EDWARD: Many that have written commendably have suppressed it or would have me publish without their names.

SIDNEY: Of which number is first that noble gentleman the Earl of Oxenforde.

EDWARD: We must have posies for our names, thus disguised we will live to write another day.

ARUNDEL: Could a Vere not tell the truth?

EDWARD: Never doubt me, nor doubt my love. My very name is truth.

(**EDWARD** *picks up another poem in manuscript.*)

EDWARD: The labouring man that tills the fertile soil
And reaps the harvest fruit, hath not indeed
The gain, but pain; and if for all his toil
He gets the straw, the lord will have the seed.
The mason poor that builds the lordly halls
Dwells not in them; they are for high degree,
His cottage is compact in paper walls,
And not with brick or stone as others be.

So he that takes the pain to pen the book
Reaps not the gifts of goodly golden muse;
But those gain that, who on the work shall look,
And from the sour the sweet by skill doth choose;
For he that beats the bush the bird not gets,
But who sits still and holdeth fast the nets.

(Lights x fade from **EDWARD** *and friends and up on* **CECIL** *and his daughter* **ANNE.**)

CECIL: This youthful parcel
Of noble bachelors stand at my bestowing
O'er whom both sovereign powers and father's voice
I have to use; thy frank election make –
Thou hast power to choose, and they none to forsake.
Peruse them well:
Not one of these but had a noble father.

(Exit **CECIL** *C.* **ANNE** *is left alone.)*

ANNE: My imagination
Carries no favour in't but Edward's
I am undone; there is as living none,
If Edward be away. T'were all one
That I should love a bright particular star
And think to wed it. He is so above me.
In his bright radiance and collateral light
Must I be comforted, not in his sphere.
The ambition in my love thus plagues itself:
The hind that would be mated by the lion
Must die for love! Twas pretty, tho' a plague
To see him every hour: to sit and draw
His arched brows, his hawking eye, his curls,
In our hearts table – heart too capable
Of every line and trick of his sweet favour.

(The light fades from her, and **CHARLES ARUNDEL** *steps into a spotlight.)*

8

ARUNDEL: (*To Audience*) My cousin the Earl of Oxford hath gotten him a wife, or at least a wife hath caught him; this is mistress Anne Cecil; whereunto the Queen hath given her consent and the which hath caused great weeping, wailing and sorrowful cheer of those that had hoped to have that golden day.

(*Movement, people gather to watch the tilt, crowd murmur and horses heard off.*)

ARUNDEL: (*cont*) There is no man of life and agility in every respect in the court but the Earl of Oxford, whose livery is crimson velvet, very costly; he himself, and the furniture is in some more colours yet he is the Red Knight!

(*Fanfare and lights change as **QUEEN ELIZABETH I** is revealed centre stage with **DAWTREY, CECIL** and **MAIDS OF HONOUR** watching the tilt, off down R. **ANNE CECIL** and **ARUNDEL** join them.*)

ARUNDEL: Fearlessly he settles himself in the saddle, gracefully bending his body this way and that. Now he circles round; now with his spurred heel he rouses his charger. The gallant animal with fiery energy collects himself together, and flying quicker than the wind beats the ground with his hoofs, and again is pulled up short as the reins control him. Bravo valiant youth! Tis thus that martial spirits pass through their apprenticeship in war. Glory already ripens thy earliest deeds!

(*Lights fade from court.*)

(*To audience.*) This triumph continued three days. The first at tilt; the second at Tournay; the third at Barriers. On every one of the challengers Her Majesty bestowed a prize, for the receiving whereof they were particularly led, armed, by the ladies, into the presence chamber;

(*Music begins under.*)

Lord Oxford himself receiving a tablet of diamonds.

(*Music swells and lights come up as **ELIZABETH** and **EDWARD** are seen dancing with others of the court. An energetic dance, after which*)

9

EDWARD *comes forward with* **SIDNEY, DAWTREY;** *the* **QUEEN** *retires upstage with her* **MAIDS OF HONOUR**.)

SIDNEY: Oh my sweet lord, that you will stay behind us!

ARUNDEL: 'Tis not his fault, the spark

YOUNG LORD: O 'tis brave wars!

SIDNEY: Most admirable! I have seen those wars.

EDWARD: I am commanded here and kept a coil with 'too young' and 'the next year and 'tis too early'.

DAWTREY: An thy mind stand to't boy, steal away bravely.

EDWARD: I shall stay here the forehorse to a smock,
Creaking my shoes on the plain masonry,
Till honour be bought up, and no sword worn
But one to dance with. By heaven I'll steal away.

SIDNEY: There's honour in the theft.

ARUNDEL: Commit it count.

YOUNG LORD: I am your accessory; and so farewell.

EDWARD: I grow to you (*they embrace*) and our parting is a tortured body.

SIDNEY: Farewell my Lord Oxford.

YOUNG LORD: What will ye do?

(*The* **QUEEN** *approaches*.)

EDWARD: Stay, the Queen!

ELIZABETH: Farewell my lords!
Those girls of Flanders, take heed of them;
They say our English lack language to deny,
If they demand; beware of being captives
Before you serve.

10

LORDS: Our hearts receive your warnings.

ELIZABETH: Farewell.

(*Exit Lords.* **EDWARD** *watches them go.* **ELIZABETH** *sits.* **ANNE CECIL** *near her.*)

EDWARD: I am minded of my father.

ELIZABETH: Thy father did look far into the service of the time and was discipled of the bravest.

EDWARD: Attired as when he walked in his own bedchamber only a dancing rapier by his side, he slew a wild boar once, while hunting near Paris. To the 'mazed French he said, "What have I done? Is it the killing of an English pig? Why every boy of my nation would have performed it. They may be bugbears to the French but to us they are servants!"

ELIZABETH: (*After a hearty laugh*) It much repairs me to talk of thy good father. So like a courtier, contempt nor bitterness were in his pride, or, if they were, his equal had awak'd them! Who were below him he used as creatures of another place, and bowed his eminent top to their low ranks making them proud of his humility. In their poor praise he humbled. Such a man might be a copy to these younger times.

EDWARD: He was a man take him for all in all, I shall not look upon his like again.

ELIZABETH: I would hear a verse.

EDWARD: I am not as I seem to be,
For when I smile I am not glad;
A thrall, although you count me free,
I, most in mirth, most pensive sad,
I smile to shade my bitter spite

11

As Hannibal that saw in sight
His country soil with Carthage town,
By Roman force defaced down.

And Caesar that presented was
With noble Pompey's princely head;
As 'twere some judge to rule the case
A flood of tears he seemed to shed;
Although indeed it sprung from joy;
Yet others thought it was annoy.
Thus contraries be used I find,
Of wise to cloak the covert mind.

I, Hannibal that smile for grief;
And let you Caesar's tears suffice;
The one that laughs at his mischief;
The other all for joy that cries.
I smile to see me scorned so,
You weep for joy to see me woe;
And I, a heart by love slain dead
Present in place of Pompey's head.

O cruel hap and hard estate
That forceth me to love my foe,
Accursed be so foul a fate,
My choice for to prefix it so.
So long to fight with secret sore
And find no secret salve therefore;
Some purge their pain by plaint I find,
But I in vain do breathe my wind.

(**ANNE CECIL** *rises but is stopped from running away.*)

ELIZABETH: Know'st thou not Edward what her father has done for me?

EDWARD: Yes, my good lady; but never hope to know why I should marry her.

ELIZABETH: Thou know'st he has rais'd a sickly kingdom.

EDWARD: But follows it, my lady, to bring me down must answer for your raising? A poor politician's daughter my wife! Disdain corrupt me ever!

ELIZABETH: 'Tis only title thou disdain'st in her, the which I can build up. Strange is it that our bloods, of colour, weight and heat, pour'd all together, would quite confound distinction, yet stand off in differences so mighty. If she be all that is virtuous – save what thou dislik'st, a poor politician's daughter, – thou dislik'st of virtue for the name, but do not so.

EDWARD: I cannot love her, nor will strive to do't.

ELIZABETH: Thou wrong'st thyself, if thou should'st strive to choose. Here take her hand, proud scornful boy, unworthy this good gift, that dost in vile misprision shackle up my love and her desert; that wilt not know it is in us to plant thine honour where we please to have it grow. Check thy contempt. Obey our will, which travails in thy good; Speak, thine answer.

EDWARD: Pardon, my gracious lady, for I submit my fancy to your eyes. When I consider what great creation and what dole of honour flies where you bid it, I find that she which late was in nobler thoughts most base is now the praised of the Queen, who so ennobled, is as 'twere born so.

ELIZABETH: Take her by the hand, and tell her she is thine.

(**ANNE CECIL** *crosses to him.*)

EDWARD: I take her hand.

ELIZABETH: Good fortune and the favour of the Queen smile upon this contract. As thou lov'st her thy love's to me religious; else does err.
(*Exit all but* **EDWARD** *and* **ARUNDEL.**)

13

EDWARD: Undone and forfeited to cares for ever!

ARUNDEL: What's the matter sweetheart?

EDWARD: Although before the solemn priest I have sworn. I will not bed her.

ARUNDEL: What, what sweetheart?

EDWARD: Oh my cousin! They have married me! I'll to the Netherland wars, and never bed her.

ARUNDEL: England is a doghole, and it no more merits the tread of a man's foot. To th' wars!

EDWARD: It shall be so; I'll write to the Queen ... that which I durst not speak. War is no strife to the dark house and the detested wife.

(The lights fade as they exit. **EDWARD** *goes to a table L. as the lights come up on a tavern. Noise of jollity offstage.* **CAPTAIN NICHOLAS DAWTREY** *a fat soldier we have seen guarding the* **QUEEN** *appears with mugs of ale. He joins* **EDWARD** *at a table.)*

DAWTREY: Is not my hostess of the tavern a most sweet wench?

EDWARD: As the honey of Hybla, my old lad of the castle. And is not a buff jerkin a most sweet robe of durance?

DAWTREY: How now, how now, mad wag! What a plague have I to do with a buff jerkin?

EDWARD: Why, what a pox have I to do with my hostess of the tavern?

DAWTREY: Well, thou hast call'd her to a reckoning many a time.

EDWARD: Did I ever call for thee to pay thy part?

DAWTREY: No, I'll give thee thy due, thou has paid all there.

EDWARD: Yea, and elsewhere, so far as my coin would stretch; and where it would not I have used my credit.

DAWTREY: Yea, and so used it that were it not here apparent
. . . 's blood thou art as melancholy as a gib cat or a
lugg'd bear.

EDWARD: Or an old lion, or a lover's lute.

DAWTREY: Yea, or the drone of a Lincolnshire bagpipe.

EDWARD: What sayest thou to a hare, or the melancholy of the
Moor Ditch?

DAWTREY: Thou hast the most unsavoury similes, and art indeed
the most comparative, rascalliest, sweet young Lord. I
would to God thou and I knew where good names were
to be bought. An old lord of the council rated me the
other day in the street about you, sir, but I mark'd him
not; and yet he talk'd very wisely, but I regarded him
not; and yet he talk'd wisely and in the street too.

EDWARD: Thou didst well; for wisdom cries out in the streets, and
no man regards it.

DAWTREY: O, thou hast damnable iteration, and art indeed able to
corrupt a saint. Thou hast done much harm upon me,
John Willie - God forgive thee for it! Before I knew thee
I knew nothing; and now am I, if a man should speak
truly, little better than one of the wicked. I must give
over this life, and I will give it over. By the lord, an I do
not I am a villain!

EDWARD: Where shall we take a purse tomorrow, old Nick?

DAWTREY: Zounds where thou wilt lad. I'll take one.

EDWARD: I see a good amendment of life in thee – from praying
to purse-taking!

DAWTREY: Why 'tis my vocation – 'tis no sin for a man to labour
in his vocation.

(*Enter* **PHILIP SIDNEY**.)

SIDNEY: My lads, my lads –

EDWARD: Good morrow Sidney

SIDNEY: Tomorrow morning, by four o'clock early at Gadshill! There are pilgrims going to Canterbury with rich offerings, and traders riding to London with fat purses. I have vizard for you all; you have horses for yourselves. I have bespoke supper tomorrow night at Eastcheap. We may do it as secure as sleep. If you will go I will stuff your purses full of crowns; if you will not, tarry at home and be hang'd.

DAWTREY: Hear ye Edward. If I tarry at home and go not, I'll hang you for going.

SIDNEY: You will, chops?

DAWTREY: Wilt thou make one?

EDWARD: Who? – I rob? I a thief? Not I by my faith.

DAWTREY: There's neither honesty, manhood, nor good fellowship in thee, nor thou cam'st not of thy father's blood if thou darest not stand for ten shillings.

EDWARD: Well then, once in my days, I'll be a madcap.

DAWTREY: Why that's well said.

EDWARD: Well, come what will, I'll tarry at home.

DAWTREY: By the lord!

SIDNEY: Sir Nicholas, I prithee, leave the Earl and me alone. I will lay him down such reasons for this adventure that he shall go.

DAWTREY: Well, God give thee the spirit of persuasion, and him the ears of profiting. Farewell, you will find me in Eastcheap.

(*Exit* **DAWTREY.**)

SIDNEY: Now, my good sweet honey lord, ride with us tomorrow. I have a jest to execute that I cannot manage alone. Dawtrey and the others shall rob those men; yourself and I will not be there; and when they have the booty, if you and I do not rob them, cut this head off from my shoulders.

EDWARD: 'Tis like that they will know us by our horses, by our habits and by every other appointment, to be ourselves.

SIDNEY: Tut! Our horses they shall not see – I'll tie them in the wood; our vizards we shall change after we leave them; and sirrah I have cases of buckram to mask our noted outward garments. The virtues of this jest will be the incomprehensible lies that this same fat rogue will tell us when we meet at supper: how thirty at least, he fought with; what wards, what blows, what extremities he endured; and in the reproof of this lives the jest.

EDWARD: Well, I'll go with thee. Provide us all things necessary, and meet me tomorrow night in Eastcheap; there I'll sup. Farewell.

SIDNEY: Farewell my lord. (*Exit* **SIDNEY.**)

EDWARD: I know you all, and will awhile uphold the unyok'd humour of your idleness; yet herein will I imitate the Sun, who doth permit the base contagious clouds to smother up his beauty from the world, that, when he please again to be himself, being wanted, he may be more wondred at by breaking through the foul and ugly mists of vapours that did seem to strangle him. If all the year were playing holidays, to sport would be as tedious as to work; but when they seldom come, they wish'd-for come, and nothing pleaseth but rare accidents. So, when this loose behaviour I throw off and pay the debt I never promised, by how much better than my word I am, by so much shall I falsify men's hopes; and like bright metal on a sullen ground, my reformation, glitt'ring o'er my fault, shall show more goodly and attract more eyes than that which hath no foil to set it off. I'll so offend to make offence a skill, redeeming time when men think least I will.

(The light fades from the tavern and up on **CECIL** *and his* **SECRETARY**, *a map of Europe is prominently displayed.)*

CECIL: *(turning from map and unrolling a map of England.)* Geographers of England jumble up haphazard in their maps imaginary sites and localities, being without art of judgement.

SECRETARY: Lawrence Nowell requests that my Lord Oxford be appointed chief cartographer, he has a talent with the pen.

CECIL: ... Canterbury ... Faunt and Wotton should return tomorrow, they have been overlong on treasurer's business.

(The lights fade and dim light is seen centre stage as **TWO TRAVELLERS** *with Cecil's emblem on their cloaks, carrying money bags appear.* **DAWTREY** *with drawn sword and* **TWO CLOAKED THIEVES** *set upon them.)*

DAWTREY: Stand!

TRAVELLERS: Jesus bless us!

DAWTREY: Strike! Down with them, out the villains' throats.

(The **THIEVES** *rob and tie up the travellers.)*

THIEVES: Bacon fed knaves!
They hate us youth. Down with them! On bacons on! What ye knaves! Young men must live.

(*Having tied their hands the* **TRAVELLERS** *are run off by* **DAWTREY** *and* **CRONIES.** **EDWARD** *and* **SIDNEY** *appear disguised.*)

EDWARD: The thieves have bound the true men. Now, could thou and I rob the thieves and go merrily to London, it would be argument for a week, laughter for a month, and a good jest for ever.

SIDNEY: Stand close; I hear them coming.

(**DAWTREY** *and* **FRIENDS** *reappear with money bags.*)

DAWTREY: Come my masters, let us share, and then to horse before day. An' the Earl and Sidney be not two arrant cowards; there's no equity stirring. There's no more valour in that lad than in a wild duck.

EDWARD: Your money!

SIDNEY: Villains!

(*They* **ALL** *run away,* **DAWTREY** *after a blow or two leaving the money behind.*)

EDWARD: Got with much ease. Now merrily to horse. The thieves are all scattered, and possess'd with fear so strongly that they dare not meet each other; each takes his fellow for an officer. Away, good Ned, Dawtrey sweats to death and lards the lean earth as he walks along. Were't not for laughing, I should pity him.

SIDNEY: How the fat rogue roar'd.

(**THEY** *exit L. Lighting change and* **CECIL** *and* **ELIZABETH** *enter in conversation from R. The* **QUEEN** *holds a letter.*)

CECIL: Your noble ward is mad. Mad I call it; for to define true madness, what is't but to be nothing else but mad? But let that go.

ELIZABETH: More matter with less art.

CECIL: Madam, 'A will come to it straight. Look you lay home to him. Tell him his pranks have been too broad to bear with, and that your Grace hath screen'd and stood between much heat and him.

ELIZABETH: (*Pause. Chooses to change the subject.*) What of the Earl of Westmoreland?

CECIL: The northern rebels hide in the low countries Ma'am with the Catholic Flemings. But Colonel Norris with several thousand men hath joined the Protestant Hollande against them, or so 'tis reported.

ELIZABETH: Nay, 'tis most credible; we here receive it, a certainty, vouched from our cousin Austria, with caution, that the Netherlands will move us for speedy aid; whereon Don John prejudicates the business, and would seem to have us make denial ...

(*Enter* **ARUNDEL** *out of breath from running, he bows.*)

... Speak Charles, if thou canst.

ARUNDEL: The Lord of Oxford and Lord Seymour are fled out of England and pass by Bruges to Brussels ...,

(**Elizabeth** *laughs long and loud, and exits L. followed by* **CECIL.** **ARUNDEL** *addresses the audience.*)

ARUNDEL: There was great triumph among the catholic rebels when they heard of the Earl of Oxford coming over; but it was full three weeks before Her Majesty sent young Master Bedingfield after them. Edward joined the Queen on a progress straight after, apparently forgiven. I think Lord Chamberlain Sussex do back him all he can. If it were not for his fickle head, he would pass any of them shortly. For the court's entertainment he penned a device named 'The Famous Victories' which told of the reigns of Harry 4 and 5 and included scenes of young Prince Hal robbing travellers on the road at Gadshill – all most fanciful but amused the Queen greatly. So that

20

at last he be granted a licence to travel abroad. Would that my Lord Burghley was so pleased!

(*Lights up on* **EDWARD** *and* **CECIL** *stage R.* **ARUNDEL'S** *spot fades as he goes L.*)

EDWARD: You make me marvel wherefore ere this time had you not fully laid my state before me, that I might so have rated my expense as I had leave of means.

CECIL: You would not hear me –

EDWARD: Go to!

CECIL: O my good lord, at many times I brought in my accounts, laid them before you; you would throw them off and say you found them in mine honesty. When for some trifling present, you have bid me return so much, I have shook my head and wept; yea, 'gainst the authority of manners pray'd you to hold your hand close. The greatest of your having lacks a half to pay your present debts.

EDWARD: Let all my land be sold.

CECIL: 'Tis all engaged, some forfeited and gone; and what remains will hardly stop the mouth of present dues.

EDWARD: To Cornwall did my land extend –

CECIL: O my good lord, the world is but a word; were it all yours to give it in a breath, how quickly were it gone!

EDWARD: You tell me true?

CECIL: If you suspect my husbandry of falsehood, call me before the exactest auditors and set me on the proof.

EDWARD: Prithee no more.

CECIL: 'Heavens' have I said 'the bounty of this lord!' How many prodigal bits have poets and actors this night engulfed! Who is not Lord Oxford's? What heart, head, sword, force, means, but is Lord Oxford's? Great Edward, noble, worthy almost royal Edward! Ah when the means are gone that buy this praise, the breath is gone whereof the praise is made. One cloud of winter showers, these flies are couched.

EDWARD: Come, sermon me no further. No villainous bounty hath yet passed my heart; unwisely, not ignobly, have I given. (*Goes to map of Europe.*)

CECIL: A traveller! By my faith you have reason to be sad. I fear you will sell your own lands to see other men's; then to have seen much and to have nothing, is to have rich eyes and poor hands.

EDWARD: Rather to see the wonders of the world abroad, than, living dully sluggardised at home, wear out my youth with shapeless idleness.

CECIL: If by travel you get a few broken languages you shall profit nothing more than to have one meat served upon divers dishes.

(**CECIL** *leaves him as the lights fade from them but stay on the map of Europe. Music is heard suggesting the French court and lights up on* **DR. DALE**, *the English Ambassador.*)

DALE: My Lord Oxford arrived in Paris this week, he did well to cumber himself with as little company as he might, two gentlemen, five grooms, a harbinger and a trenchman. Travelling as his steward is a great mathematician, philosopher, traveller and poet, Nicholas Hill, he is so eminent for knowledge and is a favourite of the great Earl. As ambassador to the French court I presented Lord Oxford unto the King and Queen, who used him honourably. Amongst other talk the King asked whether he was married. I said he had a fair lady. 'Il y

a donc, se dit-il, un beau couple.' Within six weeks my
Lord received letters from Lord Burghley ....

(*Lights up on* **EDWARD** *at writing table.*)

EDWARD: (*reading over a letter he has just written*) My lord your
letters have made me a glad man. I thank God that
it hath pleased Him to make me a father where your
lordship is a grandfather and if it be a boy I shall
likewise be the partaker with you in a greater content.
But thereby to take an occasion to return I am off from
that opinion; for now it hath pleased God to give me
a son of my own (as I hope it is) methinks I have the
better occasion to travel, whatsoever becometh of me
I leave behind me one to supply my duty and service
either to my Queen or else my country.

(*Lights X fade on to* **ANNE DE VERE** *with a small, new book.*
ARUNDEL *is with her and* **ROWLAND YORKE** *hovers near them.*)

ANNE: (*reading the dedication*) To the illustrious Lady Anne
de Vere, Countess of Oxford, while her noble husband
Edward Vere, Earl of Oxford was occupied in foreign
travel . . . .

ARUNDEL: (*reading*) Words of truth are fitting for a Vere ...
Therefore since thou, a Vere, art wife and mother of a
Vere daughter and seeing that thou mayst with good
hope look forward to being the mother of an heir of the
Veres, may thy mind always glow with love of the truth
and may thy motto be – Ever lover of the truth.

(*Lights X fade as* **ARUNDEL** *and* **ROWLAND YORKE** *exchange a
look.* **DR. DALE** *reappears in the French court.*)

DALE: Many things I have omitted to speak of which I have
heard and noted. In the city of Palermo, a thing worthy
of memory, where the Earl of Oxford, a famous man
of chivalry, made a challenge against all manner of

persons whatsoever in and at all manner of weapons, as Tournaments, Barriers with horse and armour, to fight a combat with any whatsoever in the defence of his Queen and country. For which he was very highly commended, and yet no man durst be so hardy to encounter with him. So that all Italy over he is acknowledged the only Chevalier and Nobleman of England. He hath visited Venice, Padua, Siena, Genoa, Milan and is now returned to Paris and hath presented a very proper, witty and significant device for our entertainment. There is now arrived from London a new steward, one Rowland Yorke, for my lord.

(**EDWARD** *and* **ROWLAND YORKE** *appear in conversation as the light fades from* **DR. DALE.**)

YORKE: I do beseech you, though I perchance am vicious in my guess, as, I confess it is my nature's plague to spy into abuses, and oft my jealousy shapes faults that are not – that your wisdom from one that so imperfectly conjects, would take no notice; nor build yourself a trouble out of his scattering and unsure observance. It were not for your quiet nor your good, nor for my manhood, honesty, or wisdom, to let you know my thoughts.

EDWARD: Zounds! What dost thou mean?

YORKE: Good name in man and woman dear my lord, is the immediate jewel of their souls: who steals my purse steals trash; 'tis something, nothing; 'twas mine, 'tis his, and has been slave to thousands; but he that filches from me my good name robs me of that which not enriches him and makes me poor indeed.

EDWARD: By heaven, I'll know thy thoughts.

YORKE: You cannot, if my heart were in your hand; nor shall not, whilst 'tis in my custody.

EDWARD: Ha!

YORKE: O, beware, my lord, of jealousy; it is the green-eyed monster which doth mock the meat it feeds on. That cuckold lives in bliss who, certain of his fate, loves not his wronger; but, O, what damned minutes tells he o'er who dotes, yet doubts, suspects, yet strongly loves!

EDWARD: Why, why is this? Think'st thou I'd make a life of jealousy to follow still the changes of the Moon with fresh suspicions? No; to be once in doubt is once to be resolv'd. No, Rowland; I'll see before I doubt; when I doubt, prove; and, on the proof, there is no more but this – away at once with love or jealousy!

YORKE: In London they do let God see the pranks they dare not show their husbands; their best conscience is not to leave undone, but keep't unknown.

EDWARD: Dost thou say so?

YORKE: When she seem'd to shake and fear your looks, she lov'd them most.

EDWARD: So she did.

YORKE: Why, go to then! She that, so young, could give out such a seeming, to seal her father's eyes up close as oak, he thought 'twas witchcraft. But I am much to blame, I humbly do beseech you of your pardon for too much loving you.

EDWARD: I am bound to thee for ever.

YORKE: I see this hath a little dash'd your spirits.

EDWARD: Not a jot, not a jot.

YORKE: I'faith I fear it has. I hope you will consider what is spoke comes from my love; but I do see you are mov'd. I am to pray you not to strain my speech to grosser issues nor to larger reach than to suspicion.

EDWARD: I will not.

YORKE: Should you do so, my lord, my speech should fall into such vile success which my thoughts aimed not. Arundel's a worthy friend – my lord I see you are moved.

EDWARD: No, not much mov'd. I do not think but my little countess is honest.

YORKE: Long live she so! And long live you to think so!

EDWARD: Farewell, farewell. If more thou dost hear let me know more; set on thy wife to observe! Leave me Rowland.

YORKE: My lord I take my leave. (*Going.*)

EDWARD: Why did I marry? This honest creature doubtless sees and knows more – much more than he unfolds.

YORKE: (*Returning.*) My lord I would I might entreat your honour to scan this thing no further; leave it to time. In the meantime let me be thought too busy in my fears – as worthy cause I have to fear I am – and hold her free, I do beseech your honour.

EDWARD: Fear not my government.

(**YORKE** *bows and finally exits,* **EDWARD** *sits to one side, head bowed.* **DALE** *reappears in a spotlight.*)

DALE: Lord Oxford returned to England. He had been abroad sixteen months and brought expensive gifts for the Queen but nothing for his wife, indeed he refused to see her or speak to Lord Burghley but went straight to the Queen.

(*Light fades from* **DALE** *and up on* **CECIL** *and* **ELIZABETH.**)

ELIZABETH: He hath confessed to me that with his cousins Henry Howard and Charles Arundel he hath made profession

26

of the Catholic faith, hath sworn, he says, and signed with them a declaration that they would do all they could for the advancement of the Popish religion.

CECIL: Lord Harry Howard is one of the greatest flatterers and calumniators that ever lived. Yet de Vere trusted him.

ELIZABETH: Your noblest natures are the most credulous. I have long known Howard and observed him, his brother lost his head for popish plotting, and now Arundel turns the subtle serpent. Edward has denounced the pair for plotting with the Spanish Ambassador.

CECIL: And is in the Tower for his pains.

ELIZABETH: For his protection. We will hear Arundel.

(**GUARDS** *bring in* **ARUNDEL**.)

CECIL: How say you to this treason? Know you are discovered by my Lord of Oxford.

ARUNDEL: (*Fearing for his life is quickly hysterical.*) To record the vices of that monstrous Earl were a labour without end; they are so many and so vile and so scandalous that it would be a shame to write them and a loss of time to read them .... I will truly decipher him and lay all his villainies to open gaze ... his impertinent and senseless lies ... he hath perjured himself a hundred times and damned himself to the pit of hell ... I will prove him a buggerer, of a boy that is his cook ... by Oxford's own confession as well as by witnesses ... I have seen this boy many a time in a sweat and I have gone in and found the beast in the same plight ... My Lord Harry saw more, and the boy confessed it unto Southwell and himself confirmed it unto Mr William Cornwallis....

CECIL: All good Catholic names.

ARUNDEL: And there was Orache the Italian boy … and he is a most notorious drunkard – in his drunken fits he is no man but a beast, sparing no woman be she never so virtuous, nor any man, be he never so honourable.

(**ELIZABETH** *waves him aside during this and* **ARUNDEL** *is dragged off to the Tower.*)

ELIZABETH: Edward is released. We must forbid the retaining of Jesuits and Massing priests, sowers of sedition and other treasonable attempts – exactly as you had advised my Lord Burghley, but I was late to see.

(**ELIZABETH** *exits. The lights fade from the court and* **EDWARD DE VERE** *walks slowly into a downstage spot.*)

EDWARD: Fram'd in the front of forlorn hope past all recovery,
I stayless stand, to abide the shock of shame and infamy.
My life, though lingring long, is lodg'd in love of
    loathsome ways;
My death delay'd to keep from life the harm of hapless
    days.
My sprites, my heart, my wit and force in deep distress
    are drowned;
The only loss of my good name is of these griefs the
    ground.

And since my mind, my wit, my head, my voice and
    tongue are weak
To utter, move, devise, conceive, sound forth, declare
    and speak
Such piercing plaints as answer might or would my
    woeful case,
Help crave I must and crave I will with tears upon my
    face,
Of all that may in heaven or hell, in earth or air be
    found,
To wail with me this loss of mine as of these griefs the
    ground.

Help gods, help saints, help sprites and powers that in
the heaven do dwell,
Help ye that are aye won't to wail, ye howling hounds of
hell;
Help man, help beasts, help birds and worms that on
earth do toil;
Help fish, help fowl that flock and feed upon the salt sea
soil;
Help echo that in the air doth flee, shrill voices to
resound
To wail this loss of my good name, as of these griefs
the ground.

(*Music up to climax and out as lights fade.* **BLACKOUT** – *house lights up.*)

End of Act One

Act Two

BLACKOUT
Lights up on a ship at sea; a tempestuous noise of thunder and lightning heard. A confused noise within: (this is the **BLACKFRIARS** *theatre.)*

VOICES:	Mercy on us! We split, we split! Farewell my wife and children! Farewell brother! We split, we split, we split!

The ship splits and sinks amid great rending sounds. (All sounds are man made and <u>not</u> electronic.)

MIRANDA (*a boy actor*) *runs on downstage and is frightened by the shipwreck.* **PROSPERO** (**EDWARD**) *in magic cloak and hook-on beard appears with 'her' as the wind dies to his command.*

EDWARD:	Be collected; No more amazement; tell your piteous heart there's no harm done.
MIRANDA:	O, woe the day!
EDWARD:	No harm. I have done nothing but in care of thee, of thee, my dear one, thee, my daughter, who art ignorant of what thou art, nought knowing of whence I am, nor that I am more better than Prospero, master of a full poor cell, and thy no greater father.
MIRANDA:	More to know did never meddle with my thoughts.
EDWARD:	'Tis time I should inform thee farther. Lend thy hand, and pluck my magic garment from me. So. (*They take the cloak off.*) Lie there my art. Wipe thou thine eyes; have comfort. The direful spectacle of the wreck, which touch'd the very virtue of compassion in thee, I have

with such provision in mine art so safely ordered that there is no soul – No, not so much perdition as an hair betid to any creature in the vessel which thou heard'st cry, which thou saw'st sink. Sit down for thou must now know farther.

MIRANDA: You have often begun to tell me what I am; but stopp'd and left me to a bootless inquisition, concluding 'Stay; not yet.'

EDWARD: The hour's now come; the very minute bids thee ope thine ear. Obey, and be attentive. Canst thou remember a time before we came unto this cell? I do not think thou canst; for then thou wast not out three years old
. . . .

MIRANDA: Certainly, sir, I can.

(*During this* **PHILIP SIDNEY** *walks down through the audience and out onto the stage.* **EDWARD** *interrupts the rehearsal, for such it is. As he does this* **JOHN LYLY** *appears from the wings with a prompt copy.*)

EDWARD: Philip?

SIDNEY: Aye my lord! Do I hear a new conceit?

EDWARD: The boys are new to their parts, we rehearse of necessity. Sit you there, we will finish ere long.

(**JOHN LYLY** *and* **PHILIP SIDNEY** *sit to one side and the play resumes.* **EDWARD** *puts on the cloak.*)

EDWARD as PROSPERO: Know thus far forth. By accident most strange bountiful fortune, now my dear lady, hath mine enemies brought to this shore; and by my prescience I find my zenith doth depend upon a most auspicious star, whose influence if now I court not, but omit, my fortunes will ever after droop. Here cease more questions; thou art inclined to sleep; 'tis a good dullness and give it way. I know thou can'st not choose.

31

(*Puts* **MIRANDA** *to sleep. Then closes his eyes and conjures up* **ARIEL**.)
Come away, servant; come; I am ready now.
Approach my Ariel. Come.

(*Enter* **ARIEL** [*boy actor*] *on a rope from the heavens.*)

ARIEL: All hail, great master! grave sir hail! I come to answer thy best pleasure; be't to fly, to swim, to dive into the fire, to ride on the curl'd clouds. To thy strong bidding task Ariel and all his quality.

(**ARIEL** *falls off the rope*, **MIRANDA** *'awakes' to have a look, and the rehearsal ends in a shambles.* **EDWARD** *puts off the cloak, takes off the beard and hands them to* **JOHN LYLY** *who sends the boys away.* **PHILIP SIDNEY** *laughs at the shambles.*)

SIDNEY: 'twill be perfection on the night!

EDWARD: 'tis never so!

SIDNEY: The Blackfriars theatre sees more of you than doth the court .... 'tis remarked on.

EDWARD: My Lord Sussex brings the Oxford boys to court full often. He would have us play my plays more than others. Know you that I am thought best among you for comedy.

SIDNEY: Will we see ourselves in the new piece? Is my Lord Burghley to be pilloried again in some new disguise? Will I be a low cutpurse or a princely hothead?

EDWARD: 'tis an entertainment; not a satire.

SIDNEY: A weaver of magic marooned on an island, wishing vengeance on his friends and relations? You made mention of a daughter of three years ....

EDWARD: I have never seen my daughter ....

SIDNEY: Who is now three years old.

(*Pause.* **EDWARD** *is affected by this last thought.*)

Sussex has been as a father to you. As Lord Chamberlain he knows that which you write is amusement for the court but on the public stage 'twould be treason. When Her Majesty took delight in your company ....

EDWARD: I amuse where I would serve.

SIDNEY: 'twas more than amusement. Lady Burghley was moved to censure the Queen for dallying with her son-in-law.

EDWARD: 'My Lord Burghley winketh at these love affairs' answered Bess (*they laugh*).

SIDNEY: She would have you back at court.

EDWARD: I have disgraced my ancient line. No office or council seat will be mine if I return.

(**JOHN LYLY** *reappears and busies himself with papers.*)

SIDNEY: Soon there is a progress through Essex to Cambridge and Norwich. It is known Her Majesty wishes your company. (**EDWARD** *is surprised and pleased.*) Lord Burghley and secretary Walsingham have striven to clear your name, but while you play the shy cock with actors and playhouses their work is undone.

EDWARD: So be it (*they embrace.*) John Lyly can run the playhouse, he already trains the boys and is itching to try his hand as a wordsmith.

(**EDWARD** *and* **SIDNEY** *exit.* **JOHN LYLY** *addresses the audience.*)

LYLY: My Lord Oxford needs must find favour and with it some money. He entered into bond for three thousand pound for the Martin Frobisher expedition to find Cathay by the North West, assured by Michael Lock of profits of £40 per ton on the gold ore. The ore is worthless.

Lock is publicly proclaimed a false accountant to the company, a cozener to my Lord of Oxford, a bankrupt knave.

(*Exit* **LYLY** *as we hear a distant fanfare. Re-enter* **PHILIP SIDNEY**, *during his lines* **ELIZABETH, attendants, EDWARD, ANN VAVASOR, THOMAS KNYVET** *enter and are seated.* **GABRIEL HARVEY** *appears and makes an address to the assembled court.*)

SIDNEY: Edward and Anne remained estranged from each other despite efforts by Burghley and members of both families. When the progress reached Cambridge the Queen and her courtiers were presented with a loyal address by Gabriel Harvey, a fellow of Trinity Hall. After Burghley, Leicester, Sir Christopher Hatton, Lord Sussex and myself, Harvey addressed Edward de Vere.

HARVEY: Thy splendid fame, great Earl, demands even more than in the case of others, the services of a poet possessing lofty eloquence. Thy merit doth not creep along the ground, nor can it be confined within the limits of a song. It is a wonder which reaches as far as the heavenly orbs. O thou hero worthy of renown, throw away the insignificant pen, throw away bloodless books, and writings that serve no useful purpose; now must the sword be brought into play, now is the time for thee to sharpen the spear and to handle great engines of war. In thy breast is noble blood, courage animates thy brow, Mars lives in thy tongue, Minerva strengthens thy right hand, within thee burns the fires of Mars. Thine eyes flash fire, thy countenance shakes a spear; who would not swear that Achilles had come to life again.

(*A ripple of applause,* **HARVEY** *bows and exits.* **ELIZABETH** *and* **KNYVET** *come forward.* **EDWARD** *and* **ANN VAVASOR** *flirt in the background.*)

ELIZABETH: If to do were as easy as to know what were good to do, chapels had been churches, and poor men's cottages princes' palaces. It is a good divine that follows his own instructions. I can easier teach twenty to follow mine own teaching. The brain may devise laws for the blood, but a hot temper leaps over a cold decree; such a hare is madness, the youth, to skip o'er the meshes of good council, the cripple! But this reasoning is not in the fashion to choose me a husband – O me, the word choose! I may neither choose whom I would, nor refuse whom I dislike; so is the will of a living daughter curbed by the will of a dead father. Is it not hard, Sir Thomas, that I cannot choose one, nor refuse none?

KNYVET: Your father was ever skillful, and clever men at their death have good inspirations.

ELIZABETH: If I live to be as old as Sibylla, I will die as chaste as Diana, unless I be obtained by the manner of my father's will.

ELIZABETH and **KNYVET** exit. **EDWARD** sits with **ANN VAVASOR** and a few others. **ANN** has a copy of the poem that **EDWARD** speaks.

EDWARD: Sitting alone upon my thoughts in melancholy mood,
In sight of sea, and at my back an ancient hoary wood
I saw a fair young lady come her secret fears to wail,
Clad all in colour of a nun, and covered with a veil.
Yet (for the day was calm and clear) I might discern her face
As one might see a damask rose hid under crystal glass.
Three times with her soft hand full hard on her left side she knocks
And sighed so sore as might have made some pity in the rocks.
From sighs and shedding amber tears into sweet song she brake
When thus the Echo answer'd her to every word she spake.

ANN: Oh heavens, who was the first that bred in me this
                fever?

(**EDWARD** *is the echo*)

        – Vere

        Who was the first that gave the wound, whose scar I
           wear for ever?

        – Vere

        What tyrant, Cupid, to my harm, usurps thy golden
           quiver?

        – Vere

        What sight first caught this heart, and can from
        bondage
           it deliver?

        – Vere

        Yet who doth most adore this wight, oh hollow caves
           tell true?

        – You

        What nymph deserves his liking best yet doth in sorrow
           rue?

        – You

        What makes him not reward good will with some
           reward or ruth?

        –Youth

        What makes him show besides his birth such pride and
           such untruth?

        – Youth

        May I his favour match with love if he my love will try?

        – Ay

        May I requite his birth with faith ? Then faithful will I
        die.

        – Ay

EDWARD: And I that know this lady will, said, Lord, how great
           a miracle,
        To hear how echo told the truth as true as Phoebus'
           oracle.

(*Laughter and applause from the others, the group breaks up and*
EDWARD *and* **ANN** *come downstage.*)

ANN: Will you publish your poems again this year my Lord?

EDWARD: The plays are taking more of my time. That is the way to catch the conscience of a court full of noble poets. That is the way to warn of Spanish plots and Scottish murders.

ANN: Raleigh penned me a verse.

EDWARD: That sanctimonious pirate!

ANN: Tis not out two years you were friends close as –

EDWARD: He was set on to watch me. I swear it. Secretary Walsingham's work there is no doubt.

(ANN *holds the poem in the flame of a candle, it burns up;* EDWARD *does not stop her.*)

ANN: (*contd. reading title of poem*) Verses made by the Earl of Oxford.

EDWARD: What's he?

ANN: I am sure you know him well enough.

EDWARD: Not I, believe me.

ANN: Did he never make you laugh?

EDWARD: I pray you, what is he?

ANN: Why, he is the Queen's jester, a very dull fool; only his gift is in devising impossible slanders; none but libertines delight in him, and the commendation is not in his wit but in his villainy; for he both pleases men and angers them, and then they laugh at him and beat him. I am sure he is in the fleet. I would he had boarded me.

EDWARD: When I know the gentleman, I'll tell him what you say.

ANN: Do, do; he'll but break a comparison or two on me; which, peradventure, not mark'd, or not laugh'd at, strikes him into melancholy; and then there's a partridge wing saved, for the fool will eat no supper that night.

(*Music. A dance begins off.*)

We must follow the leaders.

EDWARD: In every good thing.

ANN (*as they go*) Nay, if they lead to any ill, I will leave them at the next turning.

(*They EXIT. Music continues under.*)

SIDNEY: Mistress Ann Vavasor, a maid of honour to Her Majesty.

(**THOMAS KNYVET** *enters from dance with a* **Servant** *who is despatched on an errand,* **KNYVET** *returns to dance.*)

Master Raleigh has written verses to her and Uncle Thomas Knyvet guards her earnestly, they are sprigs of the Howard/Arundel tree that would still have revenge on my Lord Oxford for discovering their papist plots to Her Majesty. But her maids of honour must be maids or widows and methinks Mistress Vavasor is neither.

(*A laugh offstage, that we know is* **ANN VAVASOR'S**. **EDWARD** *enters.*)

EDWARD: If women could be fair and yet not fond,
Or that their love were firm, not fickle still,
I would not marvel that they make men bond,
By service long to purchase their good will;
But when I see how frail those creatures are,
I muse that men forget themselves so far.

To mark the choice they make, and how they change.
How oft from Phoebus they do flee to Pan,
Unsettled still like haggards wild they range,
These gentle birds that fly from man to man;
Who would not scorn and shake them from the fist
And let them fly fair fools which way they list?

Yet for disport we fawn and flatter both,
To pass the time when nothing else can please,
And train them to our lure with subtle oath,
Till, weary of their wiles, ourselves we ease;
And then we say when we their fancy try,
To play with fools, O what a fool was I.

SIDNEY: Alas, poor Edward, he is already dead! Stabbed with a white wench's black eye; shot through the ear with a lovesong; the very pin of his heart cleft with the blind bow-boy's buttshaft: and is he a man to encounter Knyvet?

EDWARD: Why, what is Tom Knyvet?

SIDNEY: More than a prince of cats, I can tell you.
O, he is the courageous captain of compliments.
He fights as you sing prick-song, keeps time, distance and proportion; rests me his minim rest, one, two, and the third in your bosom; and the very butcher of a silk button, a duellist; a duellist; a gentleman of the very first house.

(**THOMAS KNYVET** appears armed, with **two armed henchmen**.)

By my head, here come the Knyvets.

EDWARD: By my heel I care not.

KNYVET: Gentlemen, a word with one of you.

EDWARD: And but one word with one of us? Couple it with something; make it a word and a blow.

KNYVET: You shall find me apt enough to that, sir, an you will give me occasion.

EDWARD: Could you not take some occasion without giving?

KNYVET: De Vere, thou consort'st with my niece.

EDWARD:	Consort! What, dost thou make us minstrels? An thou make minstrels of us, look to hear nothing but discords; here's my fiddlestick; (*throws down dancing rapier*) here's that shall make you dance. Zounds, consort!
SIDNEY:	We talk here in the public haunt of men: Either withdraw unto some private place, and reason coldly of your grievances, or else depart; here all eyes gaze on us.
EDWARD:	Men's eyes were made to look, and let them gaze; I will not budge for no man's pleasure, I.
KNYVET:	De Vere, the hate I bear thee can afford no better term than this; Thou art a villain.
EDWARD:	Knyvet the reason that I have to love thee doth much excuse the appertaining rage to such a greeting. Villain am I none; therefore farewell; I see thou knowst me not.
KNYVET:	Boy, this shall not excuse the injuries that thou hast done to me; therefore turn and draw.
EDWARD:	I do protest I never injur'd thee, but love thee better than thou can'st devise till thou shalt know the reason of my love; and so, good Knyvet – which name I tender as dearly as mine own – be satisfied.
SIDNEY:	O calm, dishonourable, vile submission. Alla stoccata carries it away (*draws*) Thomas, you rat-catcher will you walk?
KNYVET:	What would'st thou have with me?
SIDNEY:	Good king of cats, nothing but one of your nine lives; that I mean to make bold withal, and, as you shall use me hereafter, dry-beat the rest of the eight. Will you pluck your sword out of his pilcher by the ears? Make haste lest mine be about your ears 'ere it be out.
KNYVET:	I am for you (*draws.*)

EDWARD: Gentle Philip, put thy rapier up.

SIDNEY: Come sir, your passado. (*Music begins under as they fight.*)

EDWARD: Gentlemen, for shame, forbear this outrage! Thomas! Philip, Her Majesty expressly hath forbid this bandying in the court. Hold, Knyvet! Good Philip.

(**EDWARD** *coming between them, is stabbed in the hip by* **KNYVET.** **KNYVET** *backs away and EXITS with henchmen.*)

I am hurt. I am sped. Is he gone and hath nothing?

SIDNEY: What, art thou hurt?

EDWARD: Ay, ay, a scratch, a scratch; marry 'tis enough. Where is my page?

SIDNEY: Courage, man; the hurt cannot be much.

EDWARD: No, 'tis not so deep as a well, nor so wide as a church door, but 'tis enough, 'twill serve.

(**SIDNEY** *helps* **EDWARD** *off. Music up to climax and diminishes under the next speech.* **JOHN LYLY** *appears and addresses the audience.*)

LYLY: As my Lord Oxford had seen ten years before in Verona, the streets of London were filled with the clamourous quarrels of these new Montagues and Capulets. For more than a year duels and ambuscades succeeded each other without interruption. During this time my lord was reconciled with his wife; finding that she had been made a fable of the world by the villainous Howard family in order to subvert him to their Catholic cause. So after six years apart they came together just as Mistress Vavasor was delivered of a son. The boy was called Edward Vere and earned his mother a cell in the Tower at the Queen's pleasure. My Lord Oxford was exiled from court for two and a half years until even Lord Burghley said he had been punished as far or farther than any like crime hath been, first by Her Majesty, and then by the drab's friend in revenge, to the peril of his life. My Lady Oxford was with child soon after and gave my lord a son that lived but two days. When the Earl of Sussex, Lord Chamberlain to the Queen, died, and the outbreak of sweating sickness closed the theatres, my Lord Oxford's company of actors travelled the country. The plays were old favourites and newer pieces and one or two of mine own. The actors were boys from the old Blackfriars' company, tragedians from the disbanded Lord Chamberlain's Company and a few poached from other noble gentlemen's patronage.

(*During this the* **ACTORS** *forming Oxford's company have gathered, including* **WILL SHAXPER**. **EDWARD** *enters leaning on a stick, which he will do for the rest of the play.*)

EDWARD: You are welcome masters; welcome all – I am glad to see thee well. – Welcome good friends – O my old friend! – Why thy face is valanced since I saw thee last; com'st thou to beard me in Coventry? What my young lady and mistress! By'r lady your ladyship is nearer to heaven than when I saw you last. Pray God your voice, like a piece of uncurrent gold, be not cracked within the ring. Masters you are all welcome. We'll e'en to't like French falconers, fly at anything we see. We'll have a speech straight. Come give us a taste of your quality; come a passionate speech.

ACTOR: However God or Fortune cast my lot,
There lives or dies, true to King Richard's throne,
A loyal, just, and upright gentleman:
Never did captive with a freer heart
Cast off his chains of bondage, and embrace
His golden –

EDWARD: Speak the speech, I pray you as I pronounced it to you, trippingly on the tongue; but if you mouth it, as many players do, I had as lief the towncrier spoke my lines. Nor do not saw the air too much with your hand, thus, but use all gently; for in the very torrent, tempest, and, as I may say, whirlwind of your passion, you must acquire and beget a temperance that may give it smoothness. O, there be players that I have seen play – and heard others praise, and that highly – not to speak it profanely, that, neither having the accent of Christians nor the gait of Christian, pagan, nor man, have so strutted and bellowed that I have thought some of nature's journeymen had made men and not made them well, they imitated humanity so abominably.

ACTOR: I hope we have reform'd that indifferently with us, sir?

EDWARD: O, reform it altogether. And let those that play your clowns speak no more than is set down for them; for there be of them that will themselves laugh, to set on some quantity of barren spectators to laugh too, though in the meantime some necessary question of the play be then to be considered. That's villainous and shows a most pitiful ambition in the fool that uses it. Go make you ready.

(**ACTORS** *exit except one young man in his early twenties, a sturdy peasant with a thick Warwickshire accent called* **WILL SHAXPER**.)

WILL: My Lord –

EDWARD: What is't Will? (*No reply: he is nervous.*) Thy name is William?

WILL: Aye sir, Will Shaxper. I've served the company for three years since ....

EDWARD: Since you – left – Sir Edward Lucy.
(*Aside to* **LYLY**) Some say wert poached from. A very excellent factotum and supernumerary actor Will. (*Embraces him.*)

WILL: (*Tongue-tied*) Sir – I would speak words.

EDWARD: Words! (*laughs*) why so you shall. What is the play tonight John Lyly?

LYLY: 'As You Like It' is preferred my lord.

EDWARD: Umm bring that rascal Audrey. (**LYLY** *exits to find him.*)

WILL: But which is the part and which the costume?

EDWARD: We will write it for you now.

WILL: For that court faction or a woodland lover am I?

EDWARD: What you will, Will!

(**WILL** *goes to the costume box and selects a hat.*)

EDWARD: Faction that ever dwells
In court where wit excels
    Hath set defiance.
Fortune and love have sworn
That they were never born
    Of one alliance.

(**JOHN LYLY** *reappears and sits to one side.*)

    Nature thought good,
    Fortune should ever dwell
    In court where wits excel,
        Love keep the wood.

(*The* **BOY playing Audrey** *appears and* **EDWARD** *takes his hand.*)

    So to the wood went I,
    With love to live and die,
        Fortunes forlorn.

    Mark this John Lyly!

(**LYLY** *attempts to copy down the following improvised scene.*)

EDWARD: Audrey, there is a youth here in the forest lays claim to you.

AUDREY: Ay, I know who 'tis, he hath no interest in me in the world, here comes the man you mean.

(*Enter* **WILL** *in an outrageous hat.*)

EDWARD: (*Aside*) It is meat and drink to me to see a clown. By my troth, we that have good wits have much to answer for: we shall be flouting; we cannot hold.

WILL: Good ev'n Audrey.

AUDREY: God ye good ev'n William.

WILL: (*Exagerated, hat-doffing bow*) And good ev'n to you sir.

EDWARD: Good ev'n, gentle friend. Cover thy head … Cover thy head; nay prithy be covered. (*Will does so at last.*) How old are you friend?

WILL: Three and twenty, sir.

EDWARD: A ripe age … is thy name William?

WILL: William, sir.

EDWARD: A fair name. Wast born in the forest here?

WILL: Ay sir, I thank God.

EDWARD: 'Thank God'. A good answer. Art rich?

WILL: Faith, sir, so so.

EDWARD: 'So so' is good very good, very excellent good; and yet it is not, it is but so so. Art thou wise?

WILL: Ay sir, I have a pretty wit.

EDWARD: Why, thou sayst well. I do now remember a saying: 'The fool doth think he is wise, but the wise man knows himself to be a fool'. The heathen philosopher, when he

45

had a desire to eat a grape, would open his lips when he put it into his mouth; meaning thereby grapes were made to eat and lips to open. You do love this maid?

WILL: I do, sir.

EDWARD: Give me your hand. Art thou learned?

WILL: No sir.

EDWARD: Then learn this of me: to have is to have; for it is a figure in rhetoric that drink, being pour'd out of a cup into a glass by filling one doth empty the other, for all your writers do consent that. Ipse dixit, now, you are not ipse, for I am he.

WILL: Which he, sir?

EDWARD: He, sir that must marry this woman.
Therefore, you clown, abandon – which is in the vulgar leave – the society – which in the boorish is company – of this female – which in the common is woman – which together is: abandon the society of this female; or clown, thou perishes; or to thy better understanding, diest; or, to wit, I kill thee, make thee away, translate thy life into death, thy liberty into bondage. Therefore tremble and depart.

AUDREY: Do, good William.

WILL: God rest you merry, sir. (**Exit WILL.**)

EDWARD: (to Lyly) The scene that will appear late in the play when he cannot but please. I will play the part of Touchstone tonight and to him William will come in the forest. You have the scene?

(**LYLY** *refers to his notes of scene just played.*)

LYLY: Good ev'n Audrey!
God Good ev'n William ….

EDWARD: If he be a quick study we could use him in other plays. Look to it John, nothing big but definitely clownish and perhaps a ghost or two.

LYLY: He will want payment, there are three children already in Stratford ….

EDWARD: Pay him! pay him John. See the players well bestowed. Do you hear? Let them be well used; for they are the abstract and brief chronicles of the time; after your death you were better have a bad epitaph than their ill report while you live.

(**EDWARD** *makes to exit then returns abstracted.*)

John Lyly, do'st remember the Frobisher expedition in '78?

LYLY: Aye, 'twas a sad winter's tale of ice and wind at gale force that drove the vessels, in spite of themselves, crashing among the bergs which were grinding and toppling on each other.

EDWARD: And of a great white bear which adventured and gave a fierce assault upon twenty men being armed. And he served them for good meat many days ….. Know you that Master Raleigh is sending a colony to this hostile land called Virginia, they will be as a new born babe on those shores.

LYLY: Bears and babes …? The terrors are exaggerated by returning travellers – sailors' yarns grow with each recital.

EDWARD: Virginia herself will not permit her new favourite to lead this expedition. She is jealous of his time, and greedy, greedy for the fairy gold found in Spanish galleons. The pirate plays the oracle while Burghley, Walsingham and Leicester are ignored and powerless. Daily grows the Spanish fleet more threatening and a Catholic Scottish Queen compounds the Popish danger.

LYLY: A play from bears and babes, colonies over the seas and hints of regicide?

EDWARD: Meat enough, John Lyly.

(*Exit* **EDWARD.** *The light x fades from* **JOHN LYLY** *and up on* **ELIZABETH** *and* **BURGHLEY**)

ELIZABETH: (*in full flood of enthusiasm for the new colony*) They are to take hot lavender, mints, savory, marjoram; the marigold that goes to bed with the sun and plant a new England in that barren land. Master Raleigh must be rewarded –

BURGHLEY: Ma'am the pressing matters –

ELIZABETH: The lands of the defeated Desmond. T'would be fitting, estates in Ireland for him. And Bedford's death means we must appoint a new Lord Warden of the Stanneries, 'tis a good income and Irish bogs yield little.

BURGHLEY: Ma'am the Scottish Queen –

ELIZABETH: I have no wish to execute my cousin.

BURGHLEY: We cannot execute without a trial and . . . .

ELIZABETH: The matter should not to come to trial. Somebody should remove the problem quietly. Often have I asked that the warrant be made unnecessary, hinting that Davison and Paulet if they loved me . . . .

BURGHLEY: There is no doubt of the love they bear your Majesty.

ELIZABETH: And my Lord Leicester where is he?

BURGHLEY: Making preparations to journey to the low countries. He has been appointed Lieutenant-General of the Queen's forces, but yesterday you –

ELIZABETH: My pleasure is that he proceed no further until he speak with me. We will send another .... Lady Oxford, is she delivered yet?

BURGHLEY: Yes Ma'am. A second daughter, Bridget – named for –

ELIZABETH: No matter. Oxford shall go as Captain of Horse to the low country wars. He has dallied with the players long enough and begs to be of service most often. The plays show he would play at politics but he does so with a fool's licence. Let him be ambassador and captain.

BURGHLEY: There are many would serve your Majesty so; Sir Philip Sidney is a worthy soldier.

ELIZABETH: A hothead. He would one day go to the New World and rides to join Drake but just as soon returns the next.

BURGHLEY: The people are curious about the cost of the New World expedition and the Forces in Flanders. The questions come daily from the country.

ELIZABETH: They do not see the Spanish threaten us from the nearest shores?

BURGHLEY: Perhaps a proclamation, a letter to your people.

ELIZABETH: No English sovereign has had need of apology. The people, my Lord Burghley, listen only to tattle in ale houses and comedians in the theatres.

BURGHLEY: Then we have the instrument to hand.

(*The lights fade from them as* **EDWARD** *and* **PHILIP SIDNEY** *stride onto the stage.*)

EDWARD: A bare six weeks abroad and I am recalled – the reason a mystery. The warlike Spaniard not a wit abashed; Her Majesty commands masquerades and comedies to be played! My purse is quite empty but still she demands and would have me send the bills to the King of Spain! Which favourite is to follow me to the breach, knowest thou Philip? (**PHILIP SIDNEY** *opens his mouth to answer.*)

Father-in-law Burghley is behind this, pouring scorn like hot oil on plays and players alike till the Queen would have us play, then fawns and scrapes the very stones ... Hast heard who so is chosen for Flanders? The players can play without a patron. There are five and twenty plays extant ....

SIDNEY: My father-in-law has received this letter of the Queen.

EDWARD: Secretary Walsingham. Spymaster general (*Taking letter*), What plot is afoot Philip? (*Reading letter*) Elizabeth ... to the Treasurer and Chamberlains of our Exchequeur. We will command you of our treasure to deliver and pay unto our right trusty and well-beloved cousin, the Earl of Oxford, or to his assigns sufficiently authorised by him, the sum of one thousand pounds good and lawful money of England. The sum to be yearly delivered at four terms of the year by even portions .... Our further will and commandment is that neither the said Earl nor his assigns shall by way of account, impress, or any other way whatsoever be charged towards us, our heirs or successors. Given under our Privy Seal at Our Manor of Greenwich, the sixth and twentieth day of June ....

SIDNEY: (*Pause*) Thou art to shake a spear at the Spaniard from the public stages Will, not in the field.

EDWARD: (*A suspicion dawns*) Who is for Flanders?

SIDNEY: Tis I.

(**JOHN LYLY** *appears in a spot.* **SIDNEY** *exits when his death is mentioned.*)

LYLY: My Lord of Oxford was immediately one of the commissioners at the trial of Mary, Queen of Scotland. Sir Philip Sidney was injured at the Battle of Zutphen and died four weeks later. Mary was condemned to death in October but was executed in February. Sir Philip died in October but was given an immense state funeral in February. Walsingham paid £6,000 of his own money toward this extraordinary spectacle. They would have us believe Sir Philip was martyred in the anti-Catholic cause and that the execution at Fotheringhay was a just punishment.

(*A drum roll as the lights change and the stage fills with activity. Music continues under as hammering and banging are heard offstage. Actors learning lines criss-cross the stage, writers and clerks in one corner, banners put up in another.*)

The group of young writers surrounding Lord Oxford at this time included Anthony Munday, Robert Greene, Thomas Kyd, Christopher Marlowe, Edmund Spenser, and myself John Lyly. Pamphlets, plays, masques and books poured forth in a patriotic stream. My Lord fitted out a ship the *Edward Bonaventure* to meet the coming invasion.

ACTOR 1. Tell me, he that knows,
Why this same strict, and most observant watch
So nightly toils the subject of the land;
And why such daily cast of brazen cannon
And foreign mart for implements of war;
Why such impress of shipwrights whose sore task
Does not divide the Sunday from the week;
What might be toward that this sweaty haste
Does make the night joint labourer with the day?

ACTOR 2. No tyrant, but a Christian King;
Unto whose grace our passion is as subject
As are our wretches fetter'd in our prisons.

(*Music bridge – build to Armada noise; lights on De Vere arms.*)

LYLY: De Vere whose fame and loyalty hath pierced
The Tuscan clime, and through the Belgike lands
By winged fame for valour is rehears't
Like warlike Mars upon the hatches stands
His tusked boar 'gan foam for inward ire
While Pallas filled his breast with warlike fire.

ACTOR 3.   Now all the youth of England are on fire
And silken dalliance in the wardrobe lies;
Now thrive the armourers, and honour's thought
Reigns solely in the breast of every man;
They sell the pasture now to buy the horse,
Following the mirror of all Christian Kings
With winged heels, as English Mercuries.
For now sits Expectation in the air,
And hides a sword from hilts unto the point
With crowns imperial, crowns and coronets,
Promised to Harry and his followers.

(*Music and noise continues under next speech.*)

ACTOR 2.   There where your argosies with portly sail,
Like signiors and rich burghers of the flood,
Or, as it were, the pageants of the sea,
Do overpeer the petty traffickers,
That curtsey to them, do them reverence
As they fly by them with their woven wings.

(*Explosions and grinding shipwrecks; as they subside the watching actors disperse.*)

ACTOR 1. (*As they go*)
I shall not see the sandy hour glass run,
But I should think of shallows and of flats,
And see my wealthy Andrew, dock'd in sand,
Vailing her high-top lower than her ribs to kiss her burial.

LYLY: (*to audience*) The Armada dispersed, the Spaniard crushed. There
was thanksgiving throughout England. The noble Earl
of Oxford the High Chamberlain of England rode right

before her Majesty, his bonnet in his hand. With the Earl Marshall he brought her to St Paul's Church, along the West Aisle to her travers in the choir, the clergy singing the litany, the two noblemen carrying a golden canopy o'er her head. At this time a third daughter was born, Susan. Ten days later the Countess died.

(*Lights x fade to a solo spot on* **EDWARD**.)

EDWARD: Sweet rose, fair flower, untimely pluck'd soon faded.
Pluck'd in the bud and faded in the spring.
Bright orient pearl, alack, too timely shaded,
Fair creature kill'd too soon by death's sharp sting
Like a green plum that hangs upon a tree
And falls through wind before the fall should be.

I weep for thee and yet no cause I have;
For why thou left me nothing in thy will
And yet thou left me more than I did crave
For why I craved nothing of thee still.
O, yes, dear friend, I pardon crave of thee
Thy discontent thou didst bequeath to me.

(*The light now reveals the young Earl of Southampton,* **HENRY WRIOTHESLEY,** *is with* **EDWARD**. **JOHN LYLY** *is still there, he is loath to speak in front of Henry.*)

LYLY: The actors do attend for rehearsal my lord.

EDWARD: What's to play, John?

LYLY: Tom Nashe has penned the piece as instructed, and the copies given out. The contention rises before the play starts with who should play the ape.

EDWARD: 'Tis the best part, or was so intended.

LYLY: They will not cover their faces.

EDWARD: 'Twere better he that personate the jackanapes be unknown ... explain the purpose John. (*Exit* **LYLY**.)
I would we were not drawn into controversy, Henry.

Know you that day and night John Lyly, Tom Nashe and others are writing pamphlets and tracts for the stage to answer Martin Marprelate.

HENRY: The mad puritan.

EDWARD: 'Tis a mystery who he is. A printing press was seized in Manchester but still his pamphlets appear. Walsingham's spies are confounded and we are now used as a mouthpiece by Burghley and church alike to answer the puritan, on his own level 'tis thought … the money has us tied … my daughter Elizabeth will come to you with no dower to speak of, my dear Henry.

HENRY: (*tongue in cheek*) Have you not lived within the bounds of your inheritance? Lord Burghley would have all wards of court increase their inheritance by prudence and careful marriages!

(**JOHN LYLY** *reappears*)

EDWARD: Truth, my Lord, to tell you plain, I can give you no other account; what I had, I have spent on good fellows; in these sports you have seen, and others of like sort.

LYLY: As giving wenches green gowns, making garlands for fencers and tricking up children gay.

EDWARD: What talk you to me of living within my bounds? I tell you, none but asses live within their bounds: the silly beasts if they be put in a pasture that is eaten bare to the very earth, will rather be hunger-starved, than they will offer to break their bounds, whereas the lusty courser breaks over hedge and ditch, e'er he will be pent in, and not have his belly full … This world is transitory; it was made of nothing, and it must to nothing; wherefore if we will do the will of our high creator – whose will it is that it pass to nothing – we must help to consume it to nothing … Tell me, I pray, wherefore was gold laid under our feet in the veins of the earth, but that we should countenance it, and tread upon it, and so consequently tread thrift under our feet? …... I thank heavens on my knees, that have made me an unthrift.

(Lighting change and music bridge under. The disbanding process i.e. the actors appear and strip props and scenery away.)

LYLY: *(To audience)* The war of the pamphlets continued. But in 1590 the company of actors known as Oxford's boys was disbanded by law, for entering controversial matters regarding Martin Marprelate and depicting him in a public place as an ape. Tom Nashe's satires were afterwards printed privately. My Lord Oxford retired and prepared his plays for publication. But first came poems dedicated to the young Earl of Southampton, Henry Wriothesley, promised in marriage at that time to his daughter, Lady Elizabeth Vere.

*(Lighting change reveals **HENRY** and **ELIZABETH** (15) chatting together upstage, and Edward apart from them in spotlight. **LYLY** exits.)*

EDWARD: When forty winters shall besiege thy brow,
And dig deep trenches in thy beauty's field,
Thy youth's proud livery, so gaz'd on now,
Will be a tatter'd weed of small worth held.
Then being asked where all thy beauty lies,
Where all the treasure of thy lusty days,
To say within thine own deep-sunken eyes
Were an all-eating shame and thriftless praise.
How much more praise deserv'd thy beauty's use,
If thou could'st answer 'this fair child of mine
Shall sum my count, and make my old excuse,'
Proving his beauty by succession thine!
This were to be new made when thou art old,
And see thy blood warm when thou feel'st it cold.

*(**ELIZABETH** runs off stage and **HENRY** wanders to table at side and picks up manuscript of collected poems.)*

HENRY: (*reading dedication*) 'To the Right Honourable Henry Wriothesley Earl of Southampton and Baron of Titchfield. The love I dedicate to your Lordship is without end: whereof this pamphlet without beginning is but a superfluous moiety. Were my worth greater my duty would show greater, meantime, as it is, it is bound to your lordship; to whom I wish long life still lengthened with all happiness. Your Lordship's in all duty. Will Shakeshaft.' William Shake-speare would be more fitting.

EDWARD: If you would have it so.

HENRY: (*Reading*) As a decrepit father takes delight
To see his active child do deeds of youth,
So I, made lame by Fortune's dearest spite,
Take all my comfort of thy worth and truth;
For whether beauty, birth, or wealth or wit,
Or any of these all, or all, or more,
Entitled in thy parts do crowned sit,
I make my love engrafted to this store.
So then I am not lame, poor, nor despis'd.

EDWARD: O lest the world should task you to recite
What merit liv'd in me, that you should love
After my death, dear love, forget me quite,
For you in me can nothing worthy prove;
Unless you would devise some virtuous lie,
To do more for me than mine own desert,
And hang more praise upon deceased I
Than niggard truth would willingly impart.
O, lest your true love may seem false in this,
That you for love speak well of me untrue,
My name be buried where my body is,
And live no more to shame nor me nor you!
For I am sham'd by that which I bring forth,
And so should you, to love things nothing worth.

(**EDWARD** *and* **HENRY** *hold positions and* **JOHN LYLY** *reappears in spot. Brief music under.*)

LYLY: My Lord Oxford remarried in retirement, this second wife was one of the Queen's maids of honour, Elizabeth Trentham, and two years later she produced the longed-for son and heir who was named Henry de Vere, Viscount Bulbec.

(**EDWARD** *and* **HENRY** *unfreeze and walk slowly away.*)

Castle Hedingham was alienated to his three daughters and the rest of his property divided between them. Elizabeth Trentham made a home for him in Hackney near to the theatres but he was never again tempted into the arena. Edmund Spenser wrote:

But that same gentle spirit from whose pen
Large streams of honey and sweet nectar flow,
Scorning the boldness of such base-born men
Which dare their follies forth so rashly show;
Doth rather choose to sit in idle cell,
Than so himself to mockery to sell.

EDWARD: (*At table*) I never am less idle, lo, then when I am alone.

LYLY: My Lord Oxford flowed with that facility that sometimes it was necessary that he be stopped. He could not crook the pregnant knee. Even when the Queen wooed he played Adonis and would not fall in. He may write to please himself but for a Lord to print verses is ridiculous and to publish them is foolish. The plays published under the name William Shakespeare earned another man fame and fortune. (*Pause music, perhaps a dance.*) With mouthing words that better wits have framed, they purchase lands and now Esquires are made.

(*The stage gradually fills with the company, first in silhouette then picked out in the light as they are referred to.* **WILL SHAXPER** *is seen during this last passage strutting and posing. At end he pauses, hand outstretched,* **HENRY WRIOTHESLEY** *puts money in it,* **LORD BURGHLEY** *is next singled out.*)

EDWARD: Robes and furr'd gowns hide all. Plate sin with gold and the strong lance of justice hurtless breaks. Arm it with rags a pigmy's straw doth pierce it.

(*Next is* **ANN VAVASOR**.)

Thine eyes I love, and they, as pitying me,
Knowing thy heart torments me with disdain,
Have put on black, and loving mourners be,
Looking with pretty ruth upon my pain.
And truly not the morning sun of heaven
Better becomes the grey cheeks of the east
Nor that full star that ushers in the even
Doth half that glory to the sober west,
As those two mourning eyes become thy face.

(*A middle-aged* **soldier** *appears near* **EDWARD**.)

Cousin Horace? Why so 'tis ....
Horatio, I am dead:
Thou liv'st; report me and my cause aright
To the unsatisfied ....
O good Horatio, what a wounded name,
Things standing thus unknown, shall live behind me!
If thou didst ever hold me in thy heart,
Absent thee from felicity awhile,
And in this harsh world draw thy breath in pain,
To tell my story.

(*The light fades from* **EDWARD**. *A final musical flourish and then lights up on full company except* **EDWARD** *and* **ELIZABETH**.)

He that played BURGHLEY:

Thus far, with rough and all-unable pen,
Our bending author hath pursu'd the story,
In little room confining mighty men,
Mangling by starts the full course of their glory.
Small time, but, in that small, most greatly lived
This Star of England.

(*Enter* **EDWARD** *without his stick.*)

EDWARD: 'Tis ten to one this play can never please
All that are here. Some come to take their ease
And sleep an act or two; but those, we fear,
W'have frightened with our trumpets; so, 'tis clear,
They'll say 'tis nought; others to hear the city
Abus'd extremely, and to cry 'that's witty!'
Which we have not done neither; that, I fear,
All the expected good w'are like to hear
For this play at this time is only in
The merciful construction of good women;
For such a one we show'd 'em. If they smile
And say 'twill do, I know within a while
All the best men are ours; for 'tis ill hap
If they hold when their ladies bid 'em clap.

(*Applause. Enter* **QUEEN ELIZABETH** *to centre stage.*)

She that plays the QUEEN:
The Queen's a beggar, now the play is done
All is well ended if this suit be won,
That you express content; which we will pay
With strife to please you, day exceeding day.
Ours be your patience then, and yours our parts;
Your gentle hands lend us, and take our hearts.

End

Appendix A

Newspaper reviews of *Nothing Truer Than Truth* performed at the Overground Theatre, Kingston-on-Thames, from 24th May to 11th June 1977.

1. *The Times* (25 May 1977) "Is there a new Bard in the House" by John Young (*see opposite*)

2. The *Guardian* (May/June 1977) "Nothing Truer Than Truth" by Tim Radford

3. *The Financial Times* (3 June 1977) "Nothing Truer than Truth" by B.A. Young

The *Richmond & Twickenham Times* (May/June 1977)

4. "Recasting the Bard" by Judy Miles

5. "Problem Play" by Judy Miles

6. "Did the 17th Earl write Shakespeare?"

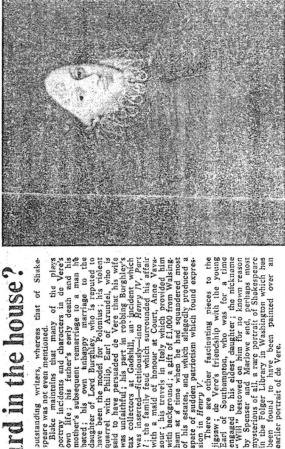

Edward de Vere : alias Shakespeare ?

Is there a new Bard in the house?

Shakespeare, as we all know, was not really Shakespeare at all. He was Christopher Marlowe, Francis Bacon, Queen Elizabeth I—or somebody else with the same name.

For those who remain convinced that the Bard's true identity has yet to be disclosed, one of the least far-fetched candidates is Edward de Vere, Seventeenth Earl of Oxford. A play about this talented, but eccentric man's life, *Nothing Truer than Truth*, opens tonight at the Overground Theatre, Kingston-upon-Thames, and its author, Darrol Blake, has assembled a mass of circumstantial evidence which, although it may well be demolished by Shakespeare scholars, at least provides an entertaining thesis.

Blake, a freelance television producer, became interested in de Vere through a meeting with Vice-Admiral Sir Ian McGeoch, who lives at Castle Hedingham, Essex, the former family seat, and through reading a book published in the 1920's by one J. Thomas Looney (a name which he admits is, in the circumstances, somewhat unfortunate).

The substance of his theory is that de Vere, although an acknowledged poet, thought it would harm his standing in Court circles if it were to be revealed that he was also a playwright, in those days considered a ruffianly trade. He therefore borrowed the name of an actor whom he had befriended and who, according to Blake, was barely literate. However, despite the use of an alias, he was evidently known to his contemporaries as the real author, since in the 1590's his name headed a list of outstanding writers, whereas that of Shakespeare was not even mentioned.

Blake maintains that many of the plays portray incidents and characters in de Vere's own life; his father's early death and his mother's subsequent remarriage to a man he hated; his own unhappy marriage to the daughter of Lord Burghley, who is reputed to have been the model for Polonius; his violent quarrel with Philip, Earl of Arundel, who is said to have persuaded de Vere that his wife was unfaithful; his part in robbing Burghley's tax collectors at Gadshill, an incident which was inserted—fictitiously—into *Henry IV, Part I*; the family feud which surrounded his affair with a maid of honour at Court, Anne Vavasour; his travels in Italy which provided him with background; a gift of £1,000 from Walsingham at a time when he had squandered most of his estates, and which allegedly produced a spate of sudden patriotism which found expression in *Henry V*.

There are other fascinating pieces to the jigsaw; de Vere's friendship with the young Earl of Southampton, who was for a time engaged to his eldest daughter; the nickname "Will" bestowed on him for no known reason by Spenser and Marlowe and, perhaps most mysterious of all, a rare portrait of Shakespeare in the Folger Library in Washington which has been found to have been painted over an earlier portrait of de Vere.

John Young

KINGSTON
Tim Radford

Nothing Truer Than Truth

THE PLAY being the thing, it matters not a whit whether or not one believes Edward de Vere, 17th Earl of Oxford, to have been the hand that penned Shakespeare. It says a lot for the Kingston Overground's extraordinary production of Nothing Truer Than Truth (the title is taken from De Vere's family motto) that after the play's two acts, you are quite prepared to believe it.

Nothing Truer Than Truth is a biographical conceit of the kind of which the Overground has made a speciality — devised, designed and directed by Darrol Blake. He has used extracts from the plays, from the poems of Oxford and other contemporary sources and arranged them into a narrative of De Vere's progress in and out of favour with the Court.

His travels abroad, his swashbuckling and literary life, his unhappy marriage, his philandering, his connection with the theatre and finally his meeting with a barely literate supernumary stagehand from Stratford-upon Avon; who might be a useful ghost (in two senses of the word) for a lord too dignified to be associated with mumming.

There are no weaknesses in the cast, the staging is deft and the costuming convincing. There is considerable attention to detail in the action : thus a young boy in women's clothes nonchalantly munches an apple between "takes" in a rehearsal sliding from urchin to Miranda as if to the mannerism born, and a career clown mums a Harpo Marx routine during Oxford's advice to his players.

Damien Thomas plays the lead with remarkable authority and Elizabethan dash ; Anne Jameson is a most credible Gloriana, both imperious and saucy.

Nothing Truer than Truth

Overground, Kingston

Whether or not there is anything in the claim considered by J. T. Looney and P. Allen that Shakespeare's works were written by Edward de Vere, 17th Earl of Oxford, it makes a jolly foundation for a theatrical caprice of the kind Darrol Blake has written and directed for the pretty little Overground Theatre in Ashdown Road, Kingston-on-Thames.

This is not to say that *Nothing Truer than Truth* (a translation of de Vere's motto) is either a very good play or a convincing warrant for the theory. It consists of a biographical study of the Earl, into which, wherever Mr. Blake has felt a connection with Shakespeare, he has introduced a passage from one of the plays to emphasise it.

For example, the youthful Oxford once robbed some Government tax collectors as a joke, and Mr. Blake has turned this into the Gadshill adventure from *Henry IV, Part I*, following it with Hal's "I know you all" speech. When Oxford has become a ward of Queen Elizabeth and continues unruly, Burghley gives here Polonius's "Your noble ward is mad", bit from *Hamlet*. There is a reflection of Othello in Oxford's jealousy over his wife, opening the way for "Who steals my purse steals trash." Oxford's wound in a sword-fight is presented as if from *Romeo and Juliet*, though he switches character from Romeo to Mercutio. There are references to *The Tempest*, *All's Well that Ends Well*, *The Winter's Tale*, and other plays, all jig-sawed into Oxford's life.

Oxford did indeed write poems and plays, though no plays have survived—not under his name, anyway. He ran two companies of players, Lord Oxford's Men at Newington Butts and Oxford's Boys, combined with the Children of the Chapel Royal, at Blackfriars. It was the latter company that was associated with John Lyly, whom Mr. Blake includes as manager and resident playwright.

But Shakespeare never played with Oxford's men as far as I know, and the suggestion that he was a bumpkin, only fit for little parts, hardly fits in with what we know of him.

Well, I don't suppose Mr. Blake is going in for serious bardology in his play. His production is very pretty to look at in its Elizabethan costumes, played on a little round open stage patterned like a chessboard, and it is fun picking up the Shakespearean allusions. Oxford himself is pleasantly if not very dashingly played by Damien Thomas and there is a striking portrait of a toughly handsome Elizabeth by Anne Jameson.

B. A. YOUNG

3. *The Financial Times* (3 June 1977) "Nothing Truer than Truth"
    by B.A. Young

Recasting the bard

WHETHER or not you think there's anything in the idea that William Shakespeare may actually have been someone else, Darrol Blake puts forward an interesting case for one contender at the Overground Theatre, Kingston.

His play Nothing Truer Than Truth (motto of the de Veres, Earls of Oxford), is couched in semi-documentary form.

It traces the career of Edward de Vere, the 17th earl, from childhood to old age, and links the events of his life with the action of the plays and the language and emotion of the sonnets.

I enjoyed it, but I'm not quite sure how clear the story—or the characters—would be to someone who was unfamiliar with them beforehand. I felt that the author, immersed in his subject, had forgotten a little the necessity of "putting it across" to the uninitiated.

It has, however, some exc llent performances. particularly from Anne Jameson—regally capricious as Queen Elizabeth I, Colin McCormack, who plays three parts, and Gary Hope who doubles as the "camp" Earl of Arundel and Sir John Lyly.

Damien Thomas, as de Vere, is both dynamic and personable. Anne Cunningham, as the "dark lady", Mistress Ann Vavasor, has the right allure and panache.

And the costumes are splendidly colourful and authentic.   **J.M.**

4.   "Recasting the Bard" by
Judy Miles
The *Richmond &*
Twickenham Times (May/
June 1977)

PROBLEM PLAY

WHO exactly was William Shakespeare?

Was he the glove-maker's son from Stratford? Was he Francis Bacon?

Or was he, as Darrol Blake believes, Edward de Vere, 17th Earl of Oxford?

Darrol's play, Nothing Truer Than Truth, currently running at the Overground, Kingston, explores the evidence supporting this theory, and the close parallels between de Vere's life and the action of the plays.

Coincidentally, it comes at a time when a sudden upsurge of "bardology" has resulted in a new novel about Shakespeare, and also a new drama series soon to be shown on television.

While a compact account of such facts of his life as are known has just been issued by the Oxford University Press.

It seems to be almost as much his year as the Queen's.

At Darrol's Barnes home he and his wife Anne talked enthusiastically of the quest for the Bard and how it all started.

Anne is involved as the mysterious Dark Lady, who emerges in the play as de Vere's mistress, Ann Vavasor. The whole business, she says, brings quite a

The Judy Miles

interview

different aspect to one's reading of Shakespeare's plays.

The sequence of events in the life of de Vere/Shakespeare are the substance of Nothing Truer Than Truth, and anyone interested will find it an intriguing and colourful evening's entertainment.

But how, I wanted to know, had Darrol come upon this idea, and why was he so convinced that "Shakespeare" really was the Earl of Oxford? "It all started," he says, "when we went on holiday to Brittany two years ago.

"There, through mutual friends, I met a leading advocate of the De-Vere-For-Shakespeare school of thought. And what he had to say was so fascinating that I felt it should be looked into further.

"Then a play which I had written about Rupert Brooke was bought for television, and this encouraged me to go back to the de Vere thing."

Darrol says that the more he read round the subject the more he was convinced that the 17th Earl might well be the true author of the greatest cycle of plays in the English language. "The thing is that everything written about the dramatist fits de Vere rather than the lad from Stratford.

"He is known to have been a clever child, and his tutor to have been the finest Latin scholar of his day.

"His father died when Edward was 12 and he became a ward of court under Burleigh.

"His mother remarried in some haste, rather like Hamlet's, and Edward's attitude to Burleigh suggests that he could have been the model for Polonius.

Balding

"There are many other incidents in his life which turn up in the plays, and what I have done is to use scenes from the plays, changing the names to their real-life ones."

Other curious facts seem to link the identities of earl and playwright.

The plays were first published by de Vere's sons-in-law, the Earl of Pembroke and the Earl of Montgomery.

One of the few authentic portraits of "Shakespeare" in the Folger Library, Washington, is painted over a portrait of de Vere. X-rays prove this, and show that the name and coat of arms have been obliterated, while the hairline has been taken back to give the familiar "balding" look.

Even more mysterious, the so-called Shakespeare monument really portrayed a fat man leaning on a

malt-sack. Various alterations were made by Garrick, the great 18th century actor, so that Shakespeare in his usual guise now appears to be resting his writing materials on a cushion.

There's a reason for the monument's original appearance, says Darrol, and it's all tied up with the origins of the pseudonym "Shakespeare". There was indeed such a person as Will Shaxper, and he was a player in the Blackfriars Theatre Company run by de Vere.

"There were two reasons why the Earl would want to preserve his anonymity," says Darrol.

Court

"Firstly, gentlemen did not publish their writings, except for court poems and Latin tags; and second someone like de Vere, who had inherited a famous title—the family had always been very close to the throne—would not be expected to consort with actors and vagabonds. Hence the actor called Shaxper was persuaded by bribes of money and land to take on the responsibility.

"When he eventually retired to Stratford he seems to have become a dealer in malt, and is known to have taken various people to court over matters connected with his business. This would explain the monument of the man leaning on a malt-sack."

De Vere's affair with Ann Vavasor, who bore him an illegitimate son, resulted in a feud between the Earl and her relatives, the Knyvetts, who were connected with the powerful Howard family; a possible source for the Montague - Capulet quarrel in Romeo and Juliet.

Darrol, who as a director has been connected with a number of well-known television series, including Doomwatch and The Onedin Line, met his Yorkshire-born wife when she was appearing in a series with Roy Kinnear.

Anne, who is now a parent manager of Westfield Primary School in Barnes, finds Mistress Vavasor, a lady with a loose reputation and an attraction for literary gents, a very credible Dark Lady. She and her husband have lived in Barnes since 1962, and she feels very involved with local life.

"The great thing about Barnes," she says, "is that it's enclosed by the common on one side and the river on two. And so it's retained its individual identity."

5. "Problem Play" by Judy Miles
The *Richmond & Twickenham Times* (May/June 1977)

Did the 17th earl write Shakespeare?

DARROL BLAKE, who has put on an Elizabethan entertainment at the Overground Theatre, Kingston, discovered that Edward de Vere, 17th Earl of Oxford, met with adventures astonishingly similar to those which form the material of the Shakespearean canon, such as junketing at the Boar's Head, snatching purses, and duelling in Verona.

As de Vere was also identified with the theatre at Blackfriars, Mr. Blake concludes that there is a good case for the theory that it was he who wrote the plays and not Bacon at all.

In a clever pastiche of quotes from the plays and sonnets, Mr. Blake puts his case dramatically, suggesting that de Vere got his pen name from an oafish Will Shaxper, brought in at the last moment to play Touchstone.

I found that the least contrived effects, in a production of much contrivance, came off best. The glittering granite of Anne Jameson's Queen Elizabeth, the statuesque authority of Dennis Edwards's Cecil, the humanity and vitality of Colin McCormack's three different roles, were not the only instances where force of personality made tricks of production rather irrelevant.

This show certainly deserves full houses for its three weeks' run. It would have been better still had the casting of Edward de Vere been a hit, not a near miss.

Damien Thomas, for all his fine voice and charm of manner, never looked like a 17th earl or the author of any works of genius. And judging by the way he swung that beer tankard about, he must be a teetotaller, thus providing little support for Mr. Blake's thesis.—RH.

"Richmond + Twickenham Times" 3/6/yy

6. "Did the 17th Earl write Shakespeare?"
The *Richmond & Twickenham Times* (May/June 1977)

Appendix B

The main passages in the play taken from the poems of Edward de Vere and others and from the Shakespeare plays and sonnets.

Act One

Page 3

The Shakespeare play: *As You Like It*, Act II sc. 7 "All the world's a stage":

EDWARD: The Stage of the World! ...

Page 4

Ovid's *Metamorphoses,* English translation by Golding/Edward de Vere:

EDWARD: *Parte tamen meliore mei (laughter and noises off)* I shall be raised immortal above the lofty stars and indelible shall be my name.

Page 5

The opening lines of the Shakespeare play: *All's Well That Ends Well,* Act I sc. 1:

COUNTESS: In delivering my son from me I bury a second husband.

EDWARD: And I in going, madam, weep o'er my father's death anew; but I must attend her Majesty's command, to whom I am now in ward, evermore in subjection.

COUNTESS: Be thou blest Edward and succeed thy father in manners as in shape! Thy blood and virtue contend for empire in thee, and thy goodness share with thy birthright! Love all, trust a few, do wrong to none, be able for thine enemy rather in power than use, and keep thy friend under thine own life's key; be checked for silence, but never tax'd for speech. What heaven more will, that thee may furnish, and my prayer pluck down, fall on thy head! Farewell. (*Edward slowly exits*)

Page 6
The Shakespeare play: *Hamlet*, Act I sc. 2
GOLDING: The funeral bak'd-meats did coldly furnish forth the marriage table.

Page 6
De Vere's poem in *Fuller Worthies Library,* Vol IV, Grosart 1872.
See also: The Shakespeare play: *Henry VI Part Three*, Act III sc. 1 "My crown is called content…"
EDWARD: Were I a King, I might command content …

Pages 7/8
De Vere's poem, Bedingfield's *Cardanus Comfort/* Richard Edwardes' *The Paradise of Dainty Devices,* 1576: see also Malim, *Great Oxford*, p.130
EDWARD: The labouring man that tills the fertile soil …

Page 8
The Shakespeare play: *All's Well That Ends Well*, Act II sc. 3
CECIL: This youthful parcel of noble bachelors stand at my bestowing …
The Shakespeare play: *All's Well That Ends Well*, Act I sc. 1
ANNE: My imagination carries no favour in't but Edward's …

Page 9
Translation of Latin verse by Giles Fletcher describing the 21-year-old Edward de Vere at a Westminster tournament in 1571. *See also* the Shakespeare play: *Henry IV Part One*, Act IV sc. 1: "I saw young Harry with his beaver on …"
ARUNDEL: Fearlessly he settles himself in the saddle …

Page 10
The Shakespeare play: *All's Well That Ends Well,* Act II sc. 1
EDWARD: I shall stay here the forehorse to a smock …
and
ELIZABETH: Those girls of Flanders take heed of them …

Pages 11/12
De Vere's poem in *The Paradise of Dainty Devices* 1576
EDWARD: I am not as I seem to be …

Pages 12/13
The Shakespeare play: *All's Well That Ends Well*, Act II sc. 3
ELIZABETH: Knowest thou ... that what her father has done for me
 ...
EDWARD: Never hope to know why I should marry her.
ELIZABETH: 'Tis only title thou disdains't in her.
EDWARD: I cannot love her ...
ELIZABETH: Thou wrong'st thyself ...

Page 14
The Shakespeare play: *All's Well That Ends Well*, Act II sc. 3
ARUNDEL: England is a doghole, and it no more merits ...
EDWARD: War is no strife to the dark house ...

The Shakespeare play: *Henry IV Part One*, Act I sc. 2
DAWTREY: Is not my hostess of the tavern a most sweet wench?
EDWARD: As the honey of Hybla ...
DAWTREY: What a plague have I to do with a buff jerkin?
EDWARD: Did I ever call for thee to play thy part?

Pages 15/16
The Shakespeare play: *Henry IV Part One*, Act I sc. 2
EDWARD: I see a good amendment of life in thee ...
DAWTREY: Tis no sin for a man to labour in his vocation ...

Pages 17/18
The Shakespeare play: *Henry IV Part One,* Act I sc. 2
EDWARD: I know you all and will awhile uphold the unyok'd
 humour ...

Pages 19/20
The Shakespeare play: *Hamlet,* Act II sc. 2
CECIL: Your noble ward is mad ...

Page 20
The Shakespeare play: *Hamlet,* Act III sc. 4
CECIL: Tell him his pranks have been too broad to bear with...

Pages 21/22

The Shakespeare play: *Timon of Athens*, Act II sc. 2

EDWARD: You make me marvel wherefore ere this time....

CECIL: O my good lord, at many times I brought in my accounts ...

EDWARD: Come, sermon me no further...

Page 22

The Shakespeare play: *As You Like It*, Act IV sc. 1 (spoken by the principal character, Rosalind, one of the Bard's great comic heroines):

CECIL: A traveller! By my faith you have reason to be sad. I fear you will sell your own lands to see other men's; then to have seen much and to have done nothing is to have rich eyes and poor hands.

Pages 24/25/26

The Shakespeare play: *Othello*, Act III sc. 3 (spoken by Iago):

YORKE: I do beseech you though I perchance am vicious in my guise, as I confess, it is my nature's plague to spy into abuses ... . Fear not my government. [Iago exits].

Page 27

Statement made by Sir Charles Arundel in his defence after being truthfully accused by Oxford of plotting against the Queen, and before being sent to the Tower and becoming the leader of the Catholic exiles in France:

ARUNDEL: To record the vices of that monstrous Earl ...

Pages 28/29

De Vere's poem, *Loss of Good Name*

EDWARD: Fram'd in the front of forlorn hope past all recovery ... O wail this loss of my good name, as of these griefs the ground. [End of Act One].

Act Two

Pages 30/31/32
The Shakespeare play: *The Tempest,* Act I sc. 2
EDWARD (as PROSPERO): Be collected. No more amazement; tell
your piteous heart there's no harm done …
to
MIRANDA: Certainly Sir, I can.

Page 34
Gabriel Harvey's address printed in *Gratulationes Valdinensis* Liber
Quartus (The Fourth Book of *Walden Rejoicing*) in 1578:
HARVEY: Thy splendid fame, great Earl, demands even more
than in the case of others …

Pages 34/35
The Shakespeare play: *The Merchant of Venice,* Act I sc 2:
ELIZABETH: If to do were as easy as to know what were good to do
…

Pages 35/36/37
De Vere's *Echo Verses*
EDWARD: Sitting alone upon my thoughts in melancholy mood
…

Page 37
The Shakespeare play: *Much Ado About Nothing,* Act II, sc. 1
ANN: Why, he is the Queen's jester [the Prince's in *Much
Ado*], a very dull fool …

Page 38
De Vere's poem (sometimes known as "Women's Changeableness")
printed in William Byrd's *Poems, Sonnets and Songs of Sadness and Piety*
in 1588:
EDWARD: If women could be fair and yet not fond …

Pages 39/40/41

Extracts from the fight dialogue between De Vere and Knyvet, which mirrors the Shakespeare play *Romeo and Juliet*, Act III sc. 1.

SIDNEY: By my head, here come the Knyvets (Capulets).

EDWARD: By my heel I care not.

KNYVET: Gentlemen, a word with one of you.

EDWARD: And but one word with one of us? Couple it with something; make it a word and a blow.

KNYVET: You shall find me apt enough to that, sir, an you will give me occasion.

EDWARD: Could you not take some occasion without giving?

KNYVET: De Vere, thou consort'st with [my niece],

EDWARD: Consort! What, dost thou make us minstrels? An thou make minstrels of us, look to hear nothing but discords; here's my fiddlestick; (*throws down dancing rapier*) here's that shall make you dance. Zounds, consort!

In the Shakespeare play, Tybalt accuses Mercutio of consorting with Romeo, and the Bard included this barb to allude to De Vere's/his own relationship with Knyvet's niece. He therefore had to invent a reason for Mercutio to take offence at the accusation, viz. "thou make minstrels of us", repeating/emphasizing "zounds, consort!"

KNYVET: Boy, this shall not excuse the injuries that thou hast done to me; therefore turn and draw.

EDWARD: I do protest I never injur'd thee, but love thee better than thou can'st devise till thou shalt know the reason of my love; and so, good Knyvet – which name I tender as dearly as mine own – be satisfied.

to

EDWARD: Gentlemen, for shame, forbear this outrage! Thomas! Philip, Her Majesty expressly hath forbid this bandying in the court. Hold, Knyvet! Good Philip.

(**EDWARD** *coming between them, is stabbed in the hip by* **KNYVET. KNYVET** *backs away and EXITS with henchmen.*)

I am hurt. I am sped. Is he gone and hath nothing?

In *Romeo and Juliet*, the Bard alluded to this royal command. Romeo says, "Tybalt! Mercutio! the Prince expressly hath forbid this bandying in Verona Streets. Hold, Tybalt! Good Mercutio!"

Pages 42/43
The Shakespeare play: *Hamlet*, Act II sc. 2
EDWARD: *(Enter the Players)* "You are welcome masters; welcome all.."

Page 44
John Dowland's madrigal in *Second Book of Songs or Ayres*
EDWARD: Faction that ever dwells …

Page 45
The Shakespeare play: *As You Like It*, Act V sc. 1
EDWARD: It is meat and drink to me to see a clown….

Pages 45/46
The Shakespeare play: *As You Like It*, Act V sc. 1
EDWARD: A ripe age … Is your name William?
WILL: Ay sir, I have a pretty wit …
EDWARD: The fool doth think he is wise …
EDWARD: Then learn this of me: to have is to have …
EDWARD: He, sir, that must marry this woman …

Page 51
The Shakespeare play: *Hamlet*, Act I sc. 5
ACTOR 1:   Tell me he that knows why this same strict, and most observant watch …

The Shakespeare play: *Henry V*, Act I sc. 2
ACTOR 2:   No tyrant, but a Christian king …

Page 52
The Shakespeare play: *Henry V*, Act II sc. 1
ACTOR 3:   Now all the youth of England are on fire ….

The Shakespeare play: *The Merchant of Venice*, Act I sc. 1
ACTOR 2:   There where your argosies with portly sail …
ACTOR 1:   I shall not see the sandy hour glass run …

Page 53
Poem X in *The Passionate Pilgrim,* 1599. Originally attributed to Shakespeare.
EDWARD: Sweet rose, fair flower, untimely pluck'd soon faded …

Page 54
Thomas Nashe's poem/entertainment 'Summer's Last Will and Testament' October 1592, published in 1600:
EDWARD: What talk you to me of living within my bounds? …

Pages 55/56
The Shakespeare Sonnet no. 2
EDWARD: When forty winters shall besiege thy brow…

The Shakespeare poem, *The Rape of Lucrece*
HENRY: (*reading dedication*) "To the Right Honorable Henry Wriothesley, Earl of Southampton and Baron Titchfield. The love I dedicate to your Lordship is without end … Your Lordship's in all duty. Will Shakeshaft." William Shake-speare would be more fitting.

The author has used dramatic licence here because the pen-name "William Shakespeare" had been used in the dedication to the Earl of Southampton in the poem, *Venus and Adonis*, which was published in the previous year.

Page 56
The Shakespeare Sonnet no. 37
HENRY: As a decrepit father takes delight …

The Shakespeare Sonnet no. 72
EDWARD: O lest the world should task you to recite …

Page 57
Edmund Spenser's poem, 'The Tears of the Muses'
LYLY: But that some gentle spirit from whose pen …

Page 58
The Shakespeare play, *King Lear*, Act IV, sc. 6
EDWARD: Robes and furr'd gowns hides all …

Pages 58
The Shakespeare Sonnet no. 132
EDWARD: Thine eyes I love ….

Page 58
The Shakespeare play: *Hamlet*, Act V sc. 2
EDWARD: Horatio I am dead ….
The Shakespeare play: *Henry V*, Act V sc. 2
BURGHLEY: Thus far, with rough and all-unable pen …

Pages 58/59
The Shakespeare play: *King Henry the Eighth*, Act V Epilogue
(supposedly written by Ben Jonson)
EDWARD: 'Tis ten to one this play can never please
                All that are here ….

Page 59
The Shakespeare play: *All's Well That Ends Well*, Act V sc. 3
ELIZABETH: The Queen's a beggar, now the play is done ….,
                All is ended if this suit is won …

Appendix C

Postscript by Oliver Kinsey

The claim that Edward de Vere, the 17th Earl of Oxford, wrote the works of Shakespeare using "William Shakespeare" as his pen-name, acted out in Darrol Blake's play, *Nothing Truer Than Truth*, is based on the investigations and discoveries detailed in schoolmaster, J. Thomas Looney's book, *Shakespeare Identified*, published in 1920. He exposed biographical material relating to de Vere's life in numerous plays of Shakespeare, including the passages set out in Appendix B for identification and ease of reference. This postscript discusses that material in two of those plays used by Darrol, and relevant events which occurred after the end of his play.

1. *All's Well That Ends Well*

The main source of *All's Well That Ends Well* was Giovanni Boccaccio's masterpiece, the *Decameron*, written in about 1350 but not published until 1470; and in *Shakespeare Identified* Mr Looney chose that play to preside largely over his biographical argument, stating that it "might indeed be compendiously described as Boccaccio's story plus the early life of Edward de Vere."[1] The *Decameron* consists of 100 novellas, short stories of love, deception and human frailties ranging from the erotic to the tragic, recounted by seven young women and three young men in Florence over ten days during the period of the Black Death[2]. That classic had a considerable influence on later works including Chaucer's *Canterbury Tales*, and of course Shakespeare, and French and English translations were published in 1545 and 1566 respectively[3].

---

1   J. Thomas Looney: *Shakespeare Identified*, Cecil Palmer (1920) pp. 223 and 233–4

2   Giovanni Boccaccio: *The Decameron* (translation by J.M. Rigg), J.M. Dent & Sons (1930) *Novel* ix, pp. 212–220

3   Naomi Magri: *All's Well That Ends Well*, Chapter 12 of *Dating Shakespeare's Plays* edited and with an Introduction and Conclusions by Kevin Gilvary,

It is likely that Edward de Vere read the *Decameron* in the 1570s, either in its original language or one or more of the above translations, and that his attention was drawn to the tale of the fictional nobleman, Bertram, the son of the Count of Rossillion because it was based on a royal wardship, and Edward was (or had been) Queen Elizabeth's first royal ward between 1562 and 1571. In the *Decameron* novella, Bertram is, on the death of his father, taken into the wardship of the French King, who forces him to marry Helena, a member of Bertram's household who loves him dearly. Bertram refuses to consummate their marriage and incurs royal disapproval by deserting his wife, travelling abroad and taking a mistress; he is tricked into sleeping with his wife who gives him a son; but in the denouement he realises the strength of her love and is reconciled with her.

Darrol's play, of course, covers Edward's royal wardship when he was placed into the household of her Chief Minister, Sir William Cecil, whose 15-year-old daughter Anne, he married on reaching his majority, and from whom he separated and took a mistress in shameful circumstances mirroring those of Bertram summarised above.[4] However, like Bertram, Edward was subsequently reconciled with his wife, and one might ask: was Edward's behaviour influenced by the *Decameron*?

All's Well That Ends Well did not appear as a play until its inclusion in the First Folio published in 1623, and there is no record of any performance of that play before 1741. Scholars have differing views as to the date when the play was most likely to have been written, based largely on allusions to contemporary events and people; but most appear to favour the period between 1590 and 1604, when Edward de Vere died.[5] I doubt that de Vere would have written the play before his wife died in 1588, nor soon after her passing, but that the birth of his son and heir in 1593 may have prompted the play's title which has mystified some commentators. Perhaps he was seeking redemption for his misdemeanours, and decided against publishing the play, or allowing it to be performed, realising the deep shame it would bring onto himself and his family, if he was identified as the author.

As we know, the manuscript of *AWTEW* passed into the possession of his daughter Susan, and she and her husband and brother-in-law

---

Parapress (2010) pp. 159–166

4   Hank Whittemore: *100 Reasons Shake-speare was the Earl of Oxford*, Forever Press USA (2016), pp. 197–200

5   Naomi Magri pp. 159–166

included that play in the First Folio without harming her family name as described below.

2. *Romeo and Juliet*

Darrol also makes telling use of *Romeo and Juliet*, which was sourced from Arthur Brooke's poem, *The Tragicall History of Romeo and Juliet*, published in 1562, and includes Edward de Vere's Echo Verses which compare closely with words which Shakespeare put into the mouth of Juliet and which are believed to allude to Edward's love affair with Ann Vavasor. Vavasor, one of the Queen's maids of honour, had been introduced to the Court by her uncle, Thomas Knyvet, a groom of the Queen's bedchamber, and her relationship with Edward had devastating consequences for both of them. It came to the Queen's attention when Vavasor bore Edward a son in early 1582, and they were both imprisoned in the Tower for three months; Edward was banned from Court for two years but his mistress's banishment and disgrace were permanent. Arthur Brooke's poem introduced the feuding Montague and Capulet families and, it is believed, gave Edward the idea of writing a play alluding to his romance with Vavasor and its aftermath. In March 1582 Knyvet (Tybalt) was provoked into challenging Edward (Romeo) to a duel in which both men were injured, and Edward was lamed for life.[6] Their quarrel was not settled, but led to frequent brawling in the streets between their servants resulting in at least one murder; and the records show that Lord Burghley urged the Queen to bring the feud to an end. Knyvet retained his honourable status, being elected a Member of Parliament for Westminster in 1584, knighted by King James I after Edward's death and elevated to the House of Lords after helping to foil the Gunpowder Plot in 1605.

Romeo and Juliet was published anonymously in 1597 and was stated to have been played publicly and often (to great applause) by (the second) Lord Hunsdon's Servants. In the previous year Hunsdon became Lord Chamberlain and his servants/players took on that name.[7] Edward de Vere might have intended that that play should remain anonymous, but Hunsdon and other courtiers would have known that he was the author. Crucially, no one but de Vere would have dared or been allowed to make those allusions to his affair with Vavasor and its consequences.

---

6   B.M. Ward: *The 17th Earl of Oxford*, John Murray (1928) p. 227
7   Gilvary, pp. 343–348

3. Edward de Vere's later life

Edward de Vere lived for 10 more years after the end of Darrol's play. In 1592 he married Elizabeth Trentham, one of the Queen's maids of honour, and their son (mentioned above) born in the next year, was surely named 'Henry' to honour the Earl of Southampton. Elizabeth provided Edward with much-needed financial support because he had lost most of his inheritance and was impecunious as a result of his extravagant lifestyle, travels and the costs of his wardship. He sought appointments from the Queen without success, but it is assumed that he continued writing and editing his plays and sonnets. He occasionally took his seat in the House of Lords, and was in 1601 a member of the tribunal which summarily tried, convicted, and sentenced to death the Earls of Essex and Southampton of treason for rebelling against the Queen; Essex was beheaded, but Southampton's sentence was commuted to life imprisonment at the behest of Sir Robert Cecil, her new Chief Minister, who argued that he had been led astray by his devotion to the Earl of Essex. It is difficult to imagine Edward's emotions at that time, but he wrote of his sadness at the death of the Queen on 24th March 1603. He suffered from frequent bouts of ill-health, but he was able to attend the coronation of King James I on 25th July and perform his inherited ceremonial role as the King's Lord Great Chamberlain.

Edward de Vere died in June 1604 and was buried in Hackney, but it is now believed that his body was subsequently reinterred in an unmarked grave in Westminster Abbey.[8] It seems likely that the King and his Privy Council agreed then with Edward's family that he would not be identified as the writer of the works of "Shakespeare" and that all necessary steps would be taken to ensure that any documents revealing such identification would be destroyed. By then, the Earl of Southampton (the only person to have been honoured with a dedication under Edward's pen-name) was a free man and being shown great favour by the King and his Queen Consort, as described below, and he too would have been privy to that agreement.

4. Henry Wriothesley, 3rd Earl of Southampton

Henry Wriothesley appears in the final scene of *Nothing Truer Than Truth* in which Darrol imagines his contribution to Edward's proposal

---

8   Alexander Waugh: *The Stratford Moniment – Revisited, De Vere Society Newsletter,* October 2014. See also the website; https://politicworm.com

to adopt a pen-name in 1593/94. That adoption (whether or not Henry was consulted) was a significant event – Edward was "crossing the Rubicon", making his dear friend Henry the figurative "custodian" of his pen-name. There is no evidence that Henry had any connection with William Shaxper of Stratford, but it seems that he was following in the footsteps of Edward de Vere (see below) and modelling his life and passions on de Vere's, and surely treasured his identification with Edward's pen-name. When he reached his 21st birthday in November 1594, he was a Cambridge graduate with "the appeal of an androgynous icon and a potentially great patron ... manly enough to fight in battle, but attractive enough to elicit delicate verses".[9] Henry then announced that he would not marry Edward's eldest daughter, Lady Elizabeth Vere, to whom he had been betrothed at the instigation of Lord Burghley. This cost him a heavy fine which together with his large wardship debts put him in desperate need of money. He was the champion of the Court at the Queen's Ascension Day festivities in 1595 but he yearned for a military career and joined his close friend, Robert Devereux, 2nd Earl of Essex (six years his senior) on several campaigns. He (like de Vere) had a secret affair with one of the Queen's maids of honour, Elizabeth Vernon (a cousin of Essex), and he lost the Queen's favour in 1598, when Vernon became pregnant and he married her.

In February 1601 (after Lord Burghley's death), the Earl of Southampton was involved (as mentioned above) in Essex's infamous rebellion. Having escaped the death penalty, he spent more than two years in prison, but, when King James VI of Scotland came to the throne of England in 1603, one of the new King's first acts was to order Henry's immediate release and pardon. Henry soon resumed his place at Court, was made a Knight of the Garter and re-created Earl of Southampton. The Queen Consort, Anne of Denmark, also showed him special favour and he entertained her at Southampton House with a performance of *Love's Labours Lost*. In 1610 he had a violent quarrel with the King's favourite, the Earl of Montgomery (see below) at tennis, but was later a supporter of Montgomery's brother, the Earl of Pembroke, in the promotion of George Villiers as a new favourite. Over the ensuing years he became a significant political figure, but was excluded from any meaningful office. He devoted much of his leisure

---

9   Park Honan: "Henry Wriothesley", *Oxford Dictionary of National Biography* (2012)

and wealth to organizing and promoting colonial enterprise; he had an up and down relationship with the King, but accompanied him on a long visit to Scotland in 1617 and two years' later was appointed to his Privy Council.

In 1621 Southampton was bitterly opposed to the King's plans to marry his son, Prince Charles, to the Spanish Infanta, Dona Maria, and was arrested for plotting mischief with members of the House of Commons and was placed in the custody of the Dean of Westminster, and the threat of that marriage was the catalyst which was to create the urgency to publish the Shakespeare plays. Also at that time, Southampton's name-sake, Henry, the 18th Earl of Oxford, Edward de Vere's son, was imprisoned in the Tower after vociferously expressing his hatred of the proposed Spanish Marriage.[10]

Henry Wriothesley, the Earl of Southampton, retained his passion for books and literature and made generous gifts to Oxford's Bodleian Library and his alma mater, St John's College, Cambridge, before he died in 1624.[11]

5. Lady Susan de Vere

Edward's youngest daughter, Lady Susan, was only 17 years old when her father died, but she was introduced to King James' Court and become a Lady-in-Waiting to the Queen Consort, Anne of Denmark; and she carried the candle for her father. On 27th December 1604, she was married to Sir Philip Herbert, aged 20, the King's favourite courtier and alleged lover, who was soon ennobled as the First Earl of Montgomery. It is recorded, not only that the King was present, but that he gave away the bride.[12] The wedding was celebrated by performances over Christmas of seven Shakespeare plays and *The Masque of Blackness* written for the occasion by Ben Jonson on the instructions of the Queen Consort. That masque was performed on Twelfth Night by the Queen Consort herself, Susan and Philip (bride and groom), and other courtiers and family members. These included her sister Lady Elizabeth de Vere, the latter's husband the 6th Earl of Derby, and Sir William Herbert, the Earl of Pembroke, Philip's elder brother who had been engaged to Edward's

10 Mark Anderson: *Shakespeare by Another Name*, Gotham Books (USA) 2005, p. 374
11 Park Honan: *ODNB*
12 Leeds Barroll: *Anna of Denmark, Queen of England, A Cultural Biography*, University of Pennsylvania Press (2001) p. 102

other daughter, Bridget. Those "royal" performances were also surely to honour of the memory of Lady Susan's father, and were evidently the beginning of a close relationship between Ben Jonson, Susan and the two Herbert brothers.[13] Jonson became the established master of masques and mysteries, and it has been claimed with authority that Jonson fell in love with Lady Susan and wrote her the most subtly erotic of poems.[14]

In 1615 her brother-in-law, William Herbert, Earl of Pembroke, achieved his great ambition, to be appointed the King's Lord Chamberlain, which gave him control of London's theatres and plays. In 1619 the London printer and bookseller, William Jaggard, who had already re-printed a number of Shakespeare plays, was positioning himself to gain access to the un-published plays and become the de facto printer of Shake-speare's works, and with this in mind dedicated a book called *The Ancient Treasury* to "the most Noble and twin-like pair" – William and Philip Herbert, and (even more graciously) to Lady Susan as the latter's wife and as daughter of the Rt. Hon. Edward de Vere, Earl of Oxenford, adding emphasis to her father's eminence by listing all his titles.[15] William and Philip were also strongly against the Spanish Marriage, not least because, if England was to become Catholic, the unpublished works of Shake-speare, gloryifying the Tudor dynasty, would probably never see the light of day.

6. The First Folio of Shakespeare's plays

In 1621, after the two Henries (Wriothesley and de Vere) had been released, *Othello* was registered for publication, the first new Shake-speare play to appear for 14 years.[16] By the end of 1622, Prince Charles and the Duke of Buckingham were preparing to go to Spain to finalise the marriage,[17] and it was time for William Jaggard to print the rest of the plays; but first they needed to be compiled and edited, and William and Philip Herbert (who were paying annuities to Ben Jonson for

---

13 Hank Whittemore, pp. 286/7
14 Adam Nicolson: *Earls of Paradise*, HarperCollins (2008) pp. xii and 180 (see also the help provided to Mr Nicolson by William Herbert, 18th Earl of Pembroke and 15th Earl of Montgomery, p. xii
15 Anderson, p. 372
16 Anderson, p. 374
17 Anderson, p. 375

services as Poet Laureate) commissioned Jonson to oversee this work[18].

The First Folio was duly published in 1623 and dedicated to William and Philip, again described as *"The Most Noble and Incomparable Paire of Brethren ... and Singular Good Lords"* although Philip did not (it appears) share his elder brother's great love of the arts. Ben Jonson put his name to the preface, addressed "To The Reader", and wrote a subtle and ambiguous epistle in memory of the author, praising his works, but deliberately supressing his identity. Jonson must have known Will Shaxsper of Stratford-upon-Avon very well as a shareholder, factotum and occasional actor of The Lord Chamberlain's Men, who had appeared in some of his own plays, and acted as the front-man for Edward de Vere's pen-name. Shaxsper had died in 1616 and the authorities had ensured that there were no burial or other records which would expose that "fronting" role or disrupt Jonson's work. As mentioned above, William Herbert, Earl of Pembroke, Lady Susan's brother-in-law, had been Lord Chamberlain with commanding authority over plays for eight years. Was this the Earl's crowning glory, and did he and Susan, who could have been Jonson's secret *"Sweet Swan of Avon"*, together vet every word of his epistle?

Lady Susan died in 1629 and was buried in Westminster Abbey, in all probability content that her father's legacy would be preserved – but not knowing for how long the identity of the writer of the works of Shake-speare would remain a mystery.

Oliver Kinsey

---

18 Anderson pp. 376–380

Index to Works